Coping with crisis

COPING WITH CRISIS
Understanding and Helping People in Need

Stephen Murgatroyd
The Open University in Wales
and The University College, Cardiff

and

Ray Woolfe
The Open University

Harper & Row, Publishers
London

Cambridge
Hagerstown
Philadelphia
New York

San Francisco
Mexico City
Sao Paulo
Sydney

Harper & Row Ltd
28 Tavistock Street
London WC2E 7PN

British Library Cataloguing in Publication Data
Murgatroyd, Stephen
   Coping with crisis.
   1. Social service – Great Britain
   I. Title II. Woolfe, Ray
361.3′0941   HV245

ISBN 0 06 318 228 9
ISBN 0 06 318 229 7 Pbk

Typeset by A-Line Services, Saffron Walden, Essex
Printed and bound in Great Britain
at The Pitman Press, Bath

About the Authors

Stephen Murgatroyd was born in Bradford and educated in Wales. He has worked as a teacher in a secondary school, as a researcher looking at counselling and learning and as a counsellor and therapist. Formerly editor of *The Counsellor*, he is a frequent contributor to the counselling literature and is now a member of the editorial board of the *British Journal of Guidance and Counselling*. For five years he co-directed counselling training programmes and has offered counselling training programmes in Canada, the USA, Norway and Britain. He is currently the Secretary of the British Psychological Society's Counselling Psychology Section.

His other publications include *Helping the Troubled Child – Interprofessional Case-Studies*, Harper & Row, 1980.

Ray Woolfe is aged 40 and is married with two children. After a period in teaching and youth work, he has worked for the past ten years as a Staff Tutor in the Faculty of Educational Studies of the Open University, based first in Cardiff and presently in Manchester. His interests include working with groups of adults concerned with self-awareness and his text *Personal Change in Adults* (with Ken Giles) forms part of an Open University course. He has qualifications in both sociology and psychology and has participated widely in programmes of counselling training. He is particularly concerned with the experience of parenthood for those who become parents of handicapped children.

To
Our Families
and
Friends

CONTENTS

Preface   xi
Introduction   1

Part One: CONCEPTS   5
1   What Is a Crisis?   7
2   What Is Coping?   22

Part Two: CRISES   39
3   Change and Development in Adult Life – A Context for Crisis   41
4   Divorce and Separation   48
5   Being Young in an Old Community – Adolescence and Crisis   63
6   Growing Old or Older and Growing – Crisis and Old Age   72
7   Parenting and Handicap – Acceptance of the Unacceptable   84
8   Unemployment – The Person and the Family   94
9   Loss and Grief   105
10   Rape   120

Part Three: COPING   135
11   Self-Help and Coping   149
12   Mutual Aid, Help and Support   156

PREFACE

A project such as this involves many persons. In our cases it has especially involved Mike Shooter, Gill Fitzgibbon, Sylvia Rhys, Camilla Lambert – fellow members of the Coping with Crisis Research and Training Group within the Open University. In addition, Mike Apter, Ken Giles, Adrienne Woolfe and Bill Law have contributed at times to our thinking. These, and many others, we especially thank.

We also thank our families and friends for being tolerant when all around was crisis – there might well have been a chapter on writing a book. Also, the Open University was especially helpful in its consideration of our needs – they even granted Steve Murgatroyd six months' leave to devote time to this (and related) projects. Marianne Lagrange and Mike Forster of Harper & Row also made more than useful contributions.

We also wish to acknowledge our clients, participants in group work and those with whom we work in community action (especially Dave Smith) for their invaluable contributions to the shaping and making of this text.

We naturally regard this text as our responsibility. We would appreciate feedback from readers. Write to The Open University in Wales, 24 Cathedral Road, Cardiff CF1 9SA or in Manchester, Charlton House, 70 Manchester Road, Manchester M21 1PQ.

Steve Murgatroyd,
Cardiff

Ray Woolfe,
Manchester

April 1982

INTRODUCTION

This text is the product of our work within the Coping with Crisis Research and Training Group of the Open University over three years. It is also the outcome of our commitment to both eclectic helping interventions within the community and with individuals and of our search for some simple models of crisis, change and transition which help in the understanding of the pain of personal crisis. We hope that this text is one which meets your needs, whatever these might be.

There are difficulties involved with the attempt to write a book about crisis experiences. Five such difficulties occur to us as we complete this project. First, the nature of crisis experiences is not widely understood. There are disputes amongst theoreticians about what is a crisis and how these events differ from, say, stressful life-events, normal developments, transition events and cathartic events (do not worry if these terms are new to you – they will become clearer later in the book). Whilst we tackle these questions in the first part of the book – a part devoted to the nature of 'crisis' and the concept of 'coping' – we will not be able to satisfy all the different theoretical schools of thought. Our pragmatism may be distressing to some.

A second difficulty concerns the aims of this text. These are: (a) to examine the concepts of crisis and coping and show how these are useful in understanding many situations of personal distress and difficulty; (b) to examine the nature of crisis events in the context of normal development; (c) to document specific examples of crisis both in terms of crisis situations (sic) and in terms of case studies; (d) to examine the structure of crisis and typical coping tactics in relation to specific situations; (e) to show the link between personal and social conditions in the generation of crisis; and finally (f) to document some steps which helpers can take – no matter what degree of experience they possess. There are too many aims, some might say, for a book of this size. Others will say that these aims lead to a book which cannot satisfy any one of them in depth. Yet our feeling and experience tells us that these are the tasks which those most concerned with crisis work wish to engage. Our task is to facilitate the exploration of these issues. This text is thus exploratory.

A further difficulty concerns the nature of the helping we envisage. Our society has become accustomed to 'helping in crisis' being regarded as the territory of professionals – doctors, social workers, district health workers, counsellors and guidance workers. Yet our experience suggests that the most imaginative and sustained group of helpers are family and friends in the majority of cases. True, professionals and para-professionals play a role in aiding some individuals and families both directly and indirectly. But there is a danger in over-investing in the skills and competences of others. We seek to make helping skills and understanding more widely available. This too may prove unpopular amongst our professional colleagues, but we feel strongly that helping is a community-wide concern and skill and that knowledge and skills need sharing widely.

The fourth difficulty associated with a text of this kind is that, because of the very nature of print as a medium, it is not possible to convey with ease the complexity, subtlety, trauma or pain of all of the individual cases which we use to illustrate key ideas, principles and practices. We trust that readers will try to project themselves into the characters we describe so as to gain a full understanding of the experience of crisis. This projection is the cornerstone of empathy – a critical helping skill. But it should be practised with caution. For it is a projection – it is not possible for you (or anyone) to fully appreciate the feelings of other persons as if they were your own. There is always the 'as if' quality.

The final difficulty we are aware of is that this text is as much about us as it is about crisis. It reflects our commitment to understanding complex personal experiences within some kind of structural framework. It reflects our commitment to a particular range of helping skills and principles. It reflects our concern to ensure that helpers working with individuals are mindful of the social consequences of their actions and of the social origins of many stressful and crisis-laden situations. The reader should be warned that there are other, different perspectives. There are other, different ways of understanding crisis and coping; other ways of interpreting crisis events and developments. We offer only what we have come to know through experience, research and reflection.

Yet reaction to this book has been interesting. Some have said that it makes the thinking about and the practice of coping with crisis accessible to a wide range of people. Others have observed that the book offers no solution to crisis experiences, but gives some elementary signposts. These reactions suggest that this book is achieving some of its aims. Our hope is that it will serve the purposes you have for it.

PART ONE: CONCEPTS

1   What Is a Crisis?

2   What Is Coping?

CHAPTER 1

WHAT IS A CRISIS?

Introduction

Different people think of a crisis in different ways. To some, a crisis occurs only rarely and will involve dramatic events externally imposed upon them, such as the death of a spouse or a close relative, rape, facial disfigurement following a motor accident, or an acute illness. For others, crises are much more frequent occurrences. They occur as the result of minor ailments or as a result of the comments or opinions voiced or written by others. When speaking about the crises of their lives, people include a variety of different experiences.

This observation leads to two points we need to make at the beginning of this book. First, the term 'crisis' cannot simply be regarded as a description of sets of circumstances or specific events. We cannot say that such and such an event *must* lead to a crisis in someone's life, since certain situations which some really do experience as a crisis would be excluded by such an approach.

Second, crises cannot be simply defined by describing events: they can only be described by reference to the ways in which individuals experience and understand such events. It is not the event of rape, or a motor accident, of being declared a bankrupt or of being diagnosed as having a terminal illness that gives rise to a crisis; it is the way people experience, think of and feel about such events which makes them crises situations.

Let us illustrate these two points by reference to some cases and let us use these cases to demonstrate their practical importance as well as their value as useful aids to our thinking.

Susan is a nineteen-year-old technical college student who was raped on her way home from college one evening. Her attacker held her at knife point, forced her to undress and then to engage in fellatio, buggery and intercourse. Jenny, a twenty-three-year-old waitress, was also raped in similar circumstances and forced to commit these same acts. Susan reported her experiences to the police and was treated by a doctor for a month for some internal injuries and by a psychiatrist for just over three years. She found subsequent relationships with men impossible to sustain. She even found her father unbearable after this event, despite having had a close and loving relationship with him previously. In contrast, Jenny did not tell anyone of her rape experience for over eleven years. For, though she had found the experience frightening for the first few minutes, she had also found the experience arousing and exciting. Indeed, the memory of her rape and the acts she was forced to commit was used by Jenny as a basis for sexual fantasies which she used during foreplay and intercourse with subsequent men friends. For Susan, the event of rape marked the beginning of a long and sustained period of crisis in her life; for Jenny, the memory of rape became a source of physical and emotional pleasure and release.

Redundancy is a much more common phenomenon than rape and is experienced by both sexes and by people of all ages. Mike and Willy were both fitters at a Welsh steel works closed during the Steel Corporation of Wales closure programme of 1979. Both were aged fifty and had worked in the works for over twenty years when their redundancies were announced. Mike found it almost impossible to cope with his situation. He became depressed and developed anorexia nervosa, losing three stone in weight in less than five months. His illness – mainly psychological – inhibited and debilitated his family life and, after eight months, his wife left him, taking with her their two youngest children. Mike was left with a thirteen-year-old daughter, who soon found herself looking after her father. Willy did not react in the same way. He used the opportunity afforded by his redundancy pay to pay off the remains of his mortgage and to take up a mature students' place at his local college. Willy has now become a careers worker and is helping many of his former colleagues to enter retraining programmes to cope with their circumstances. Willy says, 'in some senses, being made redundant was the best thing that happened since my marriage', for he has found himself developing some new skills and enjoying his circumstances – a new experience. For Willy, redundancy appears to have been a vehicle for liberation; for Mike and his family it marked the beginning of a major crisis.

These brief descriptions of the cases of Mike and Willy and of Susan and Jenny support the point that it is not the events (like rape or redundancy) which constitute a crisis, but the way in which the person experiences and thinks about these events which make them crisis-laden. They also show that different people react to similar events in different ways. Some, like Susan and Mike, require considerable help and support to cope with their situation; others, like Jenny and Willy, seek little (if any) help in similar circumstances.

Crisis Circumstances

So far we have found that crises are not easy to define objectively. We can't say that all women who experience rape or all people who experience redundancy will undergo a crisis. All we can say for sure is that some may do so and it would be foolish to argue that events such as these do not contain the potential for crisis. Our argument, however, is that to understand fully the nature of crisis, we must move beyond the event into examining the person's perception of what has happened in order to fully understand what the idea of crisis means. Another way of thinking about this idea is to use the notion of threshold level. There is plenty of evidence to suggest that some life-events such as rape, redundancy, death of a spouse, divorce, separation, illness or injury, sexual or occupational problems, birth of a handicapped child and so on are frequently associated with stress in individuals and that, beyond a certain level, this may lead to a crisis. However, the threshold level is not the same for everybody, which implies that an adequate definition of crisis must incorporate a statement about how an individual comes to terms with the event in question.

This clearly suggests that in talking about a crisis we are referring not to an event or product but to a *process*. This consists of, on the one hand, the event and, on the other hand, the person's perception of that event and his ability to develop coping strategies to deal with it. The idea of crisis as process is pursued by Brandon who says that a crisis is 'a transitional period' in a person's life which presents the individual with, on the one hand, 'an opportunity for personal growth or maturation' and, on the other, 'a risk of adverse effect with increased vulnerability to subsequent threat'. In other words, it's a process of responding to circumstances which can result *either* in an improvement in the way a person feels about himself (what we will call an improved feeling of self-esteem) *or* a failure of nerve resulting in the individual feeling worthless, unable to cope and vulnerable. This process is a crisis so long as the risk of failing in the way described here is present.

The situations which can produce this 'win' or 'lose' risk that is at the hub of the feeling that the events are crisis-laden can be of many types. We tend to think of them as unexpected calamities and of course many do fit this description. But this is not universally so, a point made by Hopson and Adams who suggest that transitional events vary according to their degree of predictability (the extent to which they can be anticipated) and voluntariness. It is interesting to apply this classification to a number of situations which we regularly associate with crisis. This allows us to articulate what the idea of crisis might mean to individuals in each situation. The concept of risk is particularly relevant to this analysis.

We all recognize the situation which is unpredictable and involuntary. It includes being subject to some criminal act (burglary, assault, robbery, rape), becoming the victim of a motor accident, losing a close relative or falling ill. The effect is that individuals suddenly find themselves exposed, at risk and possibly feeling unable to cope. But not all crisis-laden events are unpredictable, even though they are involuntary. The position our steel workers, Mike and Willy, found themselves in was that they knew their jobs were to end. Yet they could do nothing to prevent this. The death of a relative or friend as a result of prolonged terminal illness also falls into this category and so too does retirement. In this situation, although there may be a particular point when an individual first learns that he is to be made redundant, or that his wife has a terminal illness or that his child is handicapped, the problem for the individual lies in coming to terms with a situation which may unfold only slowly. In this case coping strategies have to deal with feelings that may only emerge and become apparent with the passage of time as the full realization of the situation dawns.

A third set of circumstances are characterized by being both unpredictable and voluntary; marital problems represent an appropriate example. Separation implies some degree of voluntariness on the part of at least one partner, yet the decision to end a marriage is one which is highly unpredictable and certainly cannot have been envisaged when the couple married. Paradoxically, therefore, the act of marriage can be said to contain the seeds of one of the severest crisis-producing situations – unpredictable yet voluntary. Here, the crisis an individual experiences may be related to the risk associated with the unpredictability of the circumstances. Finally and perhaps surprisingly, some circumstances can be regarded as both voluntary and predictable. One example of this is the crises that result from being a voluntary worker in a helping agency, like the Samaritans or Marriage Guidance. Becoming such a worker is a

Replace

voluntary act. In training to work in these agencies, volunteers soon become aware that helping others to cope with their crises soon results in various crises of their own, such as self-doubt, anguish and the feeling that helping may result in a particular person 'winning' or 'losing'. In other words, helping involves a crisis risk, not at all unlike the crisis risk experienced by the person seeking help.

It would seem then that crises come in many shapes and in many forms, but that in each situation the condition of crisis relates to (a) the perception an individual has of the circumstances; (b) the feeling of risk the circumstances create in the individual; (c) the feeling that, somehow, the individual has to find a way of coping with the circumstances so as to 'win' rather than lose; (d) the feeling that some action is needed, whether or not the individual knows what action to take or feels able to take that action.

The Crisis Process

Given that crisis is best perceived as a process, we are faced with the question of articulating its nature and being more specific about the cognitive and affective processes which characterize the person going through a crisis. In doing this we think it is helpful to differentiate between the concepts of crisis and stress. The latter is usually perceived in a rather pejorative fashion as having what Rapoport refers to as 'patho-genic' rather than growth-promoting potential. We agree with her and with earlier writers on crisis such as W. I. Thomas in perceiving crisis as a catalyst that disturbs old habits, evokes the potential for new responses and provides the opportunity for personal growth and development. Unlike stress, which invokes tension and anxiety, crisis is seen as bringing forward a challenge to test the efficacy of existing coping mechanisms and to discover new and more effective ones, thus leading to the possibility of improved mental health.

How then are these coping mechanisms activated? The conventional explanation lies in terms of homeostasis. This refers to the idea of equilibrium being a fundamental feature of most psychological processes and human action. So for example, individuals seek to avoid states of hunger by eating or isolation by making social contacts. In other words they are motivated by a desire to avoid uncomfortably extreme situations (a theory of drive reduction) and to maintain stress and anxiety at tolerable levels. This model of human behaviour allows us to define crisis as an upset to a stable position of equilibrium leading to subsequent attempts to achieve a new position of balance. The fact that the new equilibrium is not necessarily the same as the old is precisely the quality which gives crisis its potential for growth.

Of particular prominence in this field is the work of Caplan, who sees crisis as an upset in a steady state or to the state of an individual who finds himself in a hazardous situation and reacts in some way or other. The latter definition is one which we find apposite. It takes account of the event, the person, the risk and the desire to act. Most important he stresses that it is not to be equated with an illness. If we look at his theory of crisis in greater detail, we find that it contains two key assumptions. The first is that individuals wish to maintain 'balance' in their lives. (In fact he uses the term '*homeostasis*' to describe this equilibrium.) Rather than shifting between extremes of, say, anger and calm, individuals seek to maintain a degree of consistency or balance in their feelings about the situations they experience.

What is more, this balance helps individuals anticipate both their reactions to situations and their expectations of them. Clearly, individuals will have different reactions to different situations. What Caplan (and many other psychologists) is suggesting is that individuals are motivated by a desire to maintain stability. Crises occur when situations are perceived as being severely disruptive of this motive.

The second assumption that permeates Caplan's thinking concerns the way individuals process arousal. One of the characteristics of the crisis process is that it involves the individual in trying to cope with ever-increasing amounts of arousal. As the situation develops, the individual perceives more and more potentially disturbing features and these perceptions arouse the individual. Increasing arousal is, for Caplan, to be equated with increased anxiety. More accurately, as the discrepancy between desired arousal and felt arousal increases, the feeling of tension the individual experiences also increases.

These two aspects of crisis theory – the motivation for stability and the frustration of this motive by arousal-tension levels – are critical to an understanding of the crisis process as Caplan documents it.

The process by which an individual perceives himself as in a crisis state involves four progressive phases. These are:

Phase one
The individual finds himself comforted by a problem (a threat, a loss, a

challenge, etc.) that poses a threat to certain of his needs. He responds to the feelings of tension such as those created by confrontation, by using the problem-solving routines he has found to be successful in what he regards as similar situations from his past. All of these 'routines' are intended to restore equilibrium and reduce the feeling of threat that he is experiencing.

Phase two

If the routine fails and the feeling that the situation is a threat to certain of his needs persists, the feeling of tenison not only persists but increases, generating feelings of helplessness and encouraging trial-and-error attempts at solving the problem – almost all of which will be new to him.

Phase three

If none of the trial-and-error attempts at problem solving are successful, the feelings of threat and tension further increase. He is encouraged by the strength of these feelings to try emergency, novel and (for him) more risky problem-solving ideas. These emergency problem-solving ideas may arise from one or more of the following realizations: (a) that the problem cannot be solved but can be coped with if he changes his goals or aspirations; (b) that the problem can be resolved if looked at in a new way so as to make it fit better into his previous experiences; *or* (c) the problem can only be solved if certain parts are dismissed and all of his energy is focused upon those elements in the situation for which some sort of solution is possible. For many, this is the 'make or break' phase.

Phase four

If all the emergency solutions tried at phase three fail and he feels helpless in the face of the problem, having tried everything, feelings of tension increase to a point above his coping threshold. These feelings of tension are so powerful that they cause a major breakdown in his psychology and he may become anxiously depressed and require a high degree of skilled help.

You should note two points about these four phases. First, each of them describes a particular *level* of crisis. Phase one is a description of a crisis which may be resolved by routine coping mechanisms; phase two is a description of a crisis which may be resolved by trying, on a trial-and-error basis, new coping strategies; at phase three, crisis may be resolved by an attempt at redefining either the situation or the motives of the individual or both; and phase four is a description of a severe state of crisis for which the individual has insufficient resources to cope.

Second, just as there are different levels of crises, so also are there styles of coping: each of the phases described above involves a different coping model. We shall examine these models in greater detail in a later chapter; the important point to note here is that there are differences in the coping responses and that these differences relate to the severity of the crisis for the individual.

As described here, this process model relates to individuals. It is a description of the way a challenging situation may develop into a severe crisis if the individual's attempts to cope with each phase of the process fail. As Parad and Caplan have pointed out, this four-phase hierarchical process model works well as a description of crisis for families and close, small, social groups. Indeed, organizational analysts are using this model to study the ways in which companies and other formal organizations (such as schools and co-operatives) respond to crisis situations.

The description of these four phases provided here is very abstract. To illustrate the phases more vividly it will be helpful for you to read the description provided of Trisha's experiences with her husband Geoff. We present this case entirely from Trisha's point of view and, wherever possible, use her words to describe her feelings and actions. To make sense of the situation you need to know that Trisha and Geoff were childhood sweethearts who married at the age of twenty-one and are now twenty-seven. Trisha's parents are best described as over-bearing – providing Trisha with a generous monthly allowance. Geoff resents their 'intervention' in his relationship with Trisha, but Trisha accepts that their motives are sincere. Geoff has a medical problem which will prevent him from being able to be a father. Trisha claims that she has never experienced an orgasm with Geoff in the six years of their marriage.

Some months before this description begins, Goeff has met Brenda. Brenda is married with two young children. Geoff is gradually becoming infatuated with Brenda but Trisha is so engrossed in her work that she does not notice the growing change in Geoff's reactions to her.

Phase one

Trisha has realized that she is gradually losing Geoff, but has not yet realized why. She feels that Geoff's 'drifting away' is a real challenge to her on a number of counts. First, she feels it challenges her status as a wife. She says, 'I feel it's like saying I'm not good enough to be his wife.' Second, she regards his drifting as a reflection upon her own sexuality: 'He must have decided that I'm not a good lay.' Finally she feels strongly that his drifting is a reaction to her commitment to her career in law. 'He doesn't like the idea that he goes to places as a relative of the successful lady lawyer.' There were other issues which came to Trisha's mind – including that of adopting a family – but these three status questions (wife, lover, worker) were foremost in her mind. All three produced tensions within her since 'the situation' challenged her motives.

Her coping attempts at this stage were directly taken from previous behaviours used where there were 'little local difficulties' in their marriage. These included: (a) making special efforts to keep the house tidy, to cook favourite meals, to discuss his job and to de-emphasize hers; (b) giving way to his sexual fetish for rubberware and oral sex – something she had resisted for years after 'experimenting' in the first year of their marriage; (c) not bringing work home, arranging to take all of her annual holiday (the first time she had taken more than ten days in four years) and planning a long holiday at his favoured location.

Whilst these strategies had minimal effects, they did not halt Geoff's drift away from Trisha. Geoff told Trisha about Brenda.

Phase two

Trisha began to feel the situation was far more complex than she first thought and that she risked losing Geoff altogether. Whenever she thought about the situation she felt tense physically (stomach tension and tiredness being the main physical indications) and she cried in private for considerable lengths of time. At times she felt that her situation was hopeless and that Geoff was bound to leave her for his 'bit on the side'. At other times she was unwilling to give in so easily and was determined to do all she could to keep Geoff.

The major strategy Trisha used at this phase, additional to those used at phase one, was one of 'openness'. She aimed to get Geoff to talk through his feelings so that she could identify his problems from his point of view in the hope of responding in a way that would then change the situation. Such openness had *not* been a feature of their marriage hitherto, so she had to pursue several tactics to open out such in-depth conversations. These included: (a) buying Geoff a copy of *Becoming Partners* by Carl Rogers in the hope that his explorations of the qualities of successful marriages would encourage Geoff to talk about what was wrong with theirs; (b) writing Geoff a long letter outlining her feelings for him and indicating her willingness to give up work if it meant they could remain married; (c) trying to talk with him about their relationship and his developing relationship with Brenda. Throughout this period, she also encouraged him to see Brenda 'to really sort out his feelings' so that he 'could make decisions about his future which were really well thought out'.

None of these tactics seemed to have much effect. Geoff continued to persuade Trisha to experiment sexually (he developed an interest in mild forms of bondage) but did not talk at any length or in any depth about his feelings for either her or Brenda. He spent increasing amounts of time in Brenda's company.

Phase three

Trisha clearly felt that she was losing. She said, 'I've tried all I know to get him to be open with me. I've even gone to bed with my feet tied together and my hands tied to the bedpost thinking it would help if I could show him that I'd do anything to keep him.' The feeling that even novel tactics had failed left her more tense and helpless than before. She looked to have aged two years in as many months and had developed a range of physical symptoms which reflected her tension. These included toothaches, backaches, earaches, as well as stomach cramps and occasionally running a high temperature.

She decided that there was only one strategy left and that was total confrontation. She said, 'If I'm going to lose him anyway then I'm going to make sure he knows that I fought.' This involved a major change in her thinking. Previously any attempt to create a feeling of threat in Geoff was to be avoided since it might drive him away.

Her tactics were pursued vigorously. They included: (a) talking to Brenda's husband (who knew nothing of the situation) so as to create difficulties for Brenda; (b) talking to Brenda directly about Geoff's sexual fetishes, including showing her polaroid pictures taken by Geoff of some of their sexual antics; (c) talking to Geoff's parents and her own parents, both of Geoff's affair with Brenda and of her attempts to keep him; (d) threatening suicide if Geoff left her; and (e) calling in the police claiming that Geoff had threatened her if she didn't perform a particular sexual act that remains illegal in Britain.

Geoff left Trisha and went to live on his own in another nearby town.

Phase four

Geoff's decision to leave and not to live with Brenda left Trisha devastated. She said that she 'felt worthless as a person, and that she was unable to cope with even ordinary routines'. Her ability to concentrate declined. She felt 'unable to face people who knew her in case they asked about Geoff or in case they knew about his leaving'. She felt 'guilt for not working harder at their marriage'. She became highly anxious and extremely depressed. She was admitted to a psychiatric unit after two suicide attempts in one week. After six months of psychiatric care (four and a half weeks as an in-patient) she gradually began to pick up the pieces of her life and moved to another area. Geoff left Britain and went to work in Europe.

This very full account of Trisha's case illuminates and hopefully clarifies Caplan's model. We present it because it took Trisha through all four stages of the model and ends with her, after having tried a whole variety of coping strategies, experiencing a severe and disturbing breakdown. Caplan's model is very useful, retrospectively, in examining the steps that led to this breakdown. It also helps us to see how cognitive and feeling states interact as the individual tries to make sense of her life.

From the examination of Trisha's case, it should be clear that not all those who experience crisis situations will go through all of the four phases Caplan describes. Under different conditions, Trisha's tactics at phase one may well have succeeded (and clearly had done so for her on previous occasions). It is for this reason that we give some emphasis above to the notion of *levels of crisis*. You may have views about Trisha as a result of reading her case. Our only observation is that Trisha's first attempt to obtain skilled help with her circumstances occurred during the fourth phase – a point we shall also refer to again later in this book – when it was most difficult to help her cope with her circumstances.

We shall return to the idea of stages or levels of crisis at a number of points in this book. We shall use the idea to help us think through the kind of counselling help which might usefully be offered to individuals in a state of crisis. However, we will not accept the idea of phases uncritically and will offer our own critique of this model in which we shall challenge its central assumption: that of homeostasis. Nevertheless, the idea of phases is extremely helpful to us in trying to understand the process of crisis development by viewing it as a continuing, dynamic process.

People in Crisis

Imagine that, on your arrival home this evening you were met by two policemen who told you that your wife or husband had been killed in a road accident and that her body had been positively identified. Horowitz suggests that there are two types of initial responses to such stressful events (if indeed such an event is perceived to be stressful – it may be liberating if the marriage was unhappy). The first of these is *denial*. 'A mistake has been made!'; 'It can't possibly be true – she may have been injured, but she can't possibly be dead', or 'I don't believe it.' You react by denying that the circumstance exists or that it is a crisis for you. An alternative initial response is termed *outcry* by Horowitz. Here you respond to the circumstance by blaming others – 'I'll kill whoever did this'; 'I'll get that lunatic' – or by demanding action – 'I want a full post-mortem so we can document just how dangerous that road is.'

Here denial and outcry are stated very crudely. Let's expand upon these reactions. Denial involves individuals in only hearing what they want to hear – giving selective attention to information. They look for an alternative pattern of information to that being provided so as to give the situation hope. They do not fully experience the 'real' world because they pay selective attention to it. In fact they often lose sight of reality at crucial times. Also their actions are characterized by frantic inactivity – they spend considerable amounts of time going around in circles repeating their denial to anyone who will listen, but they are not capable of taking appropriate action since to do so would be to accept the reality of the situation and end the denial.

Outcry is a more straightforward reaction to describe. The individual perceives an injustice to have been done and seeks to collect all relevant information that supports this notion. The fact of the event is accepted – the causes of the event are questioned. This sometimes leads to a vindictiveness in the response of the individual but often gives rise to elation when evidence supporting the outcry is forthcoming and/or to tension.

In some cases, individuals begin by reacting with denial and then move to react with outcry. In other cases denial follows outcry. Yet others will react by alternating between these two responses. In all of these circumstances the process of reaction begins with a period of numbness followed by some response.

In terms of the constructs so far in this chapter, these two reactions – demand and outcry – reflect coping processes: they are ways of seeing and dealing with the event. The event itself can be examined by reference to the conditions 'involuntary-unpredictable' and responses are at the first level of Caplan's model. Notice too that (a) the crisis condition which leads to these kinds of responses depends upon the perception the individual has of the circumstances – if the death is a relief rather than a tragedy, acceptance rather than denial or outcry may well be the first response; (b) the situation does create a feeling of risk in most of those we (and Horowitz and others) have seen – they feel that they are risking their life-style by accepting the death; (c) all individuals who have encountered this circumstance feel strongly, for some time at least, that they have to find a way of coping with their new circumstances; and (d) 'denial' or 'outcry' or other responses often reflect the individual's feeling that some sort of action is needed on their part – the fact that it may not seem constructive to others should not obscure the fact that such responses are actions of some considerable importance to those who perform them.

Reactions to such events sometimes begin and end with outcry or denial, but this is rarely the case. After a while *intrusion* begins to take place. The feeling of risk, the desire to cope and the need for further action all begin to require more of a response than we have so far documented. Such thoughts often arrive at moments of exhaustion or at moments of insight and occasionally at moments of panic. But they generally do arise. Intrusion occurs when the person sees his own responses as not constructive.

Intrusion most usefully leads to a period of *working out*, during which the individual examines his reactions to date, looks critically at his situation, examines possible courses of action and acts. This working-out period can be crucial to the attempt to convert a crisis into a managed accomplishment of some kind. It is intended to lower tension and restore stability. Individuals do not always respond to intrusion in this constructive way. Sometimes the reaction is to avoid working-out and to avoid changing response; sometimes the individual feels overwhelmed and seeks refuge in self-pity or in attempting to change his emotional state by drugs or alcohol. In the framework of Caplan's model described above, working-out is the beginning of the first phase and ends when either resolution of the crisis occurs (at whatever level) or when the person finally realizes that the crisis, for him, is unresolvable. The ending of the working-out period is referred to as *completion*. These responses to a crisis event, described more fully by Horowitz, are representations of the actions people actually take when faced with a significant threat or challenge. Horowitz provides a framework through which we can study people in crisis; their ability to cope and the effects of the crisis upon their lives. We can ask: if this same crisis event occurred again, will this individual be better equipped to cope? Will the response to this crisis help the individual to respond to other situations? How has the individual changed?

Crisis: Good and Bad

In this book several cases have already been presented. Some were unable to respond to their crisis event in such a way as to secure an outcome that was beneficial to them. Others not only coped with their crises but learned from them and became stronger as a result. For others, it is still (even after a number of years) too soon to tell if they are to benefit from the experience of their crisis or if they are to be changed in ways undesirable to them as a result of their crisis events.

The fact that crises involve this risk – individuals can *either* learn from crises (we call this personal growth or transition learning) *or* be undesirably changed (we called this 'being scarred') by crises – has led some to argue that crises are both inevitable and *necessary* to personal growth. Bertram Forer, a psychiatrist, is one who suggests this. He argues that, with many of the individuals he has helped, their working-out of their reactions to crisis events has lead to: (a) the individual being less prone to crisis events; (b) the individual being better prepared for future crises; (c) the individual feeling less vulnerable; (d) changed self-esteem and greater respect for the self-esteem of others; (e) the individual being more objective in his view of the environment and his relationships with others; and (f) the individual being more open with others. He suggests that, for those who resolve their crises, these outcomes arose only because of that crisis – they would not have arisen in any other way. On the basis of this observation he argues that crises are necessary to personal growth.

We do not accept this view. Whilst it is true that some people can only learn about themselves when forced by crisis events to do so, it is a large step to move on to argue that therefore everyone should have crises in their lives.

The point we wish to make at the end of this chapter is simple. Crises events *can* become most productive for personal growth. The kinds of outcomes documented by Forer are possible in a large number of cases. The task of those who seek to help individuals who are experiencing crises is to make that experience as productive in terms of personal growth as possible. Equally important for helpers is the task of minimizing the extent to which the individual is 'scarred' by their experience of their crisis. Both of these are difficult, complex tasks. Inevitably helpers will fail and the scars will be extensive and deep. These failures constitute the helpers' crises.

CHAPTER 2

WHAT IS COPING?

Introduction

Just as it is necessary to explore the meaning of the term 'crisis' and to understand the implications of being 'in crisis' for the persons experiencing a crisis situation and for those who wish to help them, so it is necessary to examine the term 'coping' and study its implications.

Richard Lazarus, a psychologist working at the University of Berkeley in California, is a key figure amongst those who study coping behaviour. In a series of books and papers he has clarified and refined the nature of coping and has studied the effectiveness of different coping strategies through careful observations of those persons experiencing stressful life-events and crisis situations. His work provides an important and essential backcloth for other work related to coping, and this chapter will reflect his thinking as well as that of many of his co-workers.

For Lazarus, coping has two functions. First, coping is concerned with changing a situation which is stressful or crisis-laden. This may be achieved either by changing the nature of the situation itself or by changing the person's reactions to the situation. A second function of coping, subtly different from the first, involves the attempt to manage or deal with our thoughts, feelings and bodily reactions under conditions of stress or crisis without necessarily trying to change ourselves or the situation in any systematic way. The first function of coping is called *change* whilst the second might be described as *management*.

Let us examine these two functions of coping by reference to some illustrative cases, presented briefly here.

Mike is a young executive in a large insurance company. He is gifted and able, but is constantly facing dismissal because of his attitude towards his superiors. He thinks and feels that Bob, his boss, is inept and incapable when it comes to making certain decisions. He bases this thought on a certain incident in which Bob did indeed make a mistake which had several undesirable consequences. This occurred when Mike and Bob were both employed at the same grade in the company, though Bob has subsequently been promoted. Mike has been warned about his attitude towards Bob and other persons holding senior positions in the company and the threat of dismissal is affecting his work and domestic life very seriously, with his wife threatening to leave if he loses his job. Mike asks to see a counsellor.

The counsellor works through Mike's thoughts and feelings about Bob and other senior staff in the company. Mike is persuaded to make a list of the strengths of the company and each person working within it, including himself. The counsellor works with Mike on his list, giving particular emphasis to: (a) the strengths and qualities of the other staff and (b) the interdependence of all staff on each other. Mike is then asked to list five key decisions each of the persons senior to him have got wrong in the last year. He can only think of one, and part of the 'blame' for this mistake rests fairly and squarely on his own shoulders.

As a result of his consultation, Mike seeks out new ways of working with his superiors, suggesting possible developments within the company. In general, he becomes less aggressive and makes more direct contributions to the thinking and planning of the company's work than he has done for some time. After two years, he is promoted and all threats of dismissal are gone. In the same time, tension at home declines and Mike remains married, despite a fear that divorce was imminent at the beginning of these stressful events.

In this situation, Mike changes the way he thinks about work and those he has to work with. His change of attitude and behaviour leads to a change in the thinking and behaviour of others, both at home and at work. That this is so is reflected both in his promotion and in the continuation of his marriage, which many (including Mike) thought to be breaking down. Mike *coped* with his situation by changing the way he thought and behaved when in it. Coping here served a change function.

Shelagh gave birth to a child with severe physical disabilities which required considerable attention on her part and repeated visits to doctors and hospitals and repeated visits from social workers, health visitors, doctors, district nurses and others.

Shelagh finds both the experience of being the mother to a severely disabled child a major crisis and the visiting very stressful, though she is determined to 'keep going, no matter what happens'. To relax, she drinks gin and tonics and smokes, but only after her child has gone to bed. Gradually she finds that she is drinking more and more and smoking an increasing number of cigarettes. By the end of the first year after the birth, Shelagh is drinking three bottles of gin each week and smoking sixty cigarettes each day. She regards this as 'the only way I can blunt the feelings that are fighting inside me'.

It may seem strange that we cite Shelagh as an example of a coping person, since her drinking and smoking behaviour may damage her health and, in the long or medium term, reduce her ability to cope with her child considerably, thus making her life more stressful and crisis-laden than it already is. It is clear, however, that Shelagh is currently managing her stress and feelings of crisis in this way. Whilst she may eventually wish or be forced to find other methods of coping, the alcohol and smoking help her cope in terms of Lazarus's management conception of coping.

The case of Shelagh leads us to make two observations about coping as a concept which are important to understand at the beginning of this chapter. First, what counts as coping in one area of a person's life may not count as coping in another. A person who copes with a crisis at work by taking it out on the family may soon be experiencing a crisis at home. Shelagh may soon experience stress in relation to her health or in relation to her feelings of dependency on both alcohol and tobacco. Nonetheless, Shelagh is coping with her feelings – at least for now. Second, the term 'coping' refers to the process of coping (in relation to change *or* management) not to whether or not this process turns out to be successful according to any objective criteria of success. Coping is thus a term used to describe a person's *attempts* to change or manage a situation, *not* whether they succeed in doing so.

A Definition of Coping

These last two observations bring us nearer to our definition of coping, borrowed here from Lazarus and Launier. Throughout this book the term 'coping' will be used to refer to a person's attempts to manage (i.e., master, tolerate, reduce, minimize, etc.) internal and environmental demands and conflicts which tax or exceed his resources. This definition sounds a little complex. Let us 'unpack' it a little.

The terms 'internal' and 'environmental' refer to the thoughts, feelings, body-responses and actions of the person in crisis, on the one hand, and to the thoughts, feelings, actions of others and the dynamics of the situation on the other. The phrase 'attempts to manage' emphasize a point already made: coping is concerned with a person's efforts to manage or change a situation which is stressful or crisis-laden to him, rather than as to whether these efforts prove to be successful. Coping thus involves a variety of thoughts and actions, as is clear from the words included in parenthesis. This means that there is not a particular way of coping with divorce or rape, for example, but a variety of ways which stem from the person's character, biography, biology and their relationships with others. Coping focuses not only upon the relationship between the person and the environment. Most important of all, coping as a term refers to a dynamic process – it is not simply a description of one-off events.

It should be clear from this definition of coping and from the discussion of coping functions which preceded it, that a large number of different coping *tactics* can be used by a person in response to stressful or crisis events. Jack Dunham of the University of Bath, for example, has documented the various tactics used by social workers to cope with their own feelings of panic or crisis which result from their work. These include: prayer, meditation, yoga, physical activities such as jogging and cycling, sharing problems and worries with someone else not involved in work and constantly (but constructively) evaluating the place of work in life. Other writers, such as Collette Ray and Gill Fitzgibbon, have documented the tactics used by people who are about to undergo surgery. Colin Murray Parkes has documented tactics used by widows in coping with bereavement. With so many different tactics available, some broader framework to make sense of and help promote coping is needed.

Such a framework is provided by Leonard Pearlin and Carmi Schooler, two psychologists working at the National Institute of Mental Health (USA). They begin by drawing a distinction between *tactics*, such as those described briefly above, and *strategy*. A strategy is the scheme a person adopts in order to cope with some specific stressful or crisis event, whilst a tactic is the person's way of implementing this scheme. For example, Mike's visit to the counsellor and completion of various lists were tactics representative of his strategy for change, whilst Shelagh's drinking and smoking were tactics which reflected her strategy for management. Pearlin and Schooler suggest that there are essentially three strategies of coping. These are: (a) strategies aimed at preventing situations developing as crises or stress – *the anticipatory strategy*; (b) strategies aimed at creating a buffer between the person and the crisis environment so as to prevent the full effects of the crisis or stress being experienced – *the buffer strategy*; and (c) the strategy of coping with a crisis event by learning to manage the feelings and thoughts experienced – *the crisis-management strategy*.

Anticipatory Coping

The first strategy documented by Pearlin and Schooler is one used by a great many people. It involves the prediction of some stressful or crisis-laden situation and the taking of action to either avoid or change the situation. Two examples will illustrate the kind of coping actions that fall into this category.

In Britain and many other countries, pregnant women are encouraged to anticipate the experience of childbirth and are taught strategies both for dealing with the pain of childbirth and for the nurturing of their child in the period immediately after birth. One strategy for dealing with pain that will be encountered during the contraction and birth period is called psycho-prophylaxis – meaning a psychological preparation for the prevention of pain. The mother-to-be is taught several tactics for dealing with pain during contractions. These tactis include relaxation techniques, specific breathing techniques and ways of diverting thoughts from the pain to some other thought (frequently a nursery rhyme). Essentially, the woman is taught to anticipate pain and to respond to it in such a way as to both reduce its impact (hence the relaxation and breathing tactics) and changes its meaning (thought diversion). For this reason, we may regard psycho-prophylaxis as an example of anticipatory coping.

A second example relates to marriage. When a couple begin to experience stress in their marriage they may anticipate a pending crisis in their realtionship and act to prevent it by means of some sort of negotiation. The aim of this negotiation is to inhibit the development of the crisis – to confront the underlying difficulty and find some amicable way of resolving it so that the marriage can continue. In a number of cases the marriage partners will themselves facilitate this negotiation, but in others the intervention of a marriage guidance counsellor or of a relative might be a prerequisite for the negotiation. Once again, a crisis situation is anticipated and action is taken to either avoid the situation or to change it.

Anticipatory coping is a common coping strategy. Its use removes the need for a great many people to seek help in the resolution of crisis situations. Their anticipatory coping is so effective that they do not experience crisis events or, if they do, it is because they were impossible to predict.

Yet studies of coping behaviours amongst those people who do experience crises suggest that anticipatory coping is not as widely used as a coping strategy as we might think. To understand why this is the case it is necessary to examine the requirements for the use of anticipatory coping. First, it requires the accurate identification of the potential source of crisis. Such recognition is not always easy. In marriage, for example, it is not always easy to find a specific feature which is in need of change so as to make the continuation of a relationship possible. Next, even when the source of potential stress is recognized, people do not always have the knowledge, skills or strengths to eliminate, modify or transform them.

The third barrier to the use of the anticipatory coping strategy is a difficulty we have already encountered in our brief look at the coping tactics used by Shelagh: the development of a coping tactic to deal with one aspect of a person's life (e.g., work) may lead to strains, stresses and crises in others (e.g., marriage). Thus the use of simple coping strategies or tactics may lead to rather than prevent crisis; this thought may effectively act to block the use of anticipatory coping. Finally, not all situations can be changed or avoided. Whilst certain difficulties may be anticipated, such as those to be faced by having a severely handicapped child, it is not always possible to affect the situation significantly and to avoid the resultant stresses or crises.

Just as it is not always possible to make a significant impact upon a situation by means of coping tactics, so is it the case that not all situations which give rise to crisis experiences can be anticipated. Rape, redundancy, serious injury in a car accident or a heart attack may not be readily amenable to the use of the anticipatory coping strategy.

Despite the difficulties associated with the use of anticipatory coping, several examples exist of attempts to teach anticipatory coping skills. The most frequently cited examples of such teachable skills are: (a) transcendental meditation and relaxation training techniques; (b) assertiveness training; and (c) transactional analysis. In addition, various skills of decision making can be learned and should be seen as examples of a certain type of anticipatory coping skill.

Transcendental meditation – TM for short – is a series of techniques used to facilitate both physical and mental relaxation, and to encourage the mind to pay total attention to the 'sounds' of the body so as to ensure that body and mind function in harmony and in the same rhythm. Using a particular body posture and a series of breathing exercises, practitioners of TM are encouraged to focus upon a particular thought (known as a mantra) to the exclusion of all other thoughts. An example of a mantra would be to attend to the sounds made by a ball of cotton wool falling to the ground repeatedly. Though sitting on the floor with legs crossed with a straight back, breathing deeply and regularly, whilst concentrating upon this thought may seem strange to others, there is strong evidence to suggest that TM does enable a person to relax at a deep level. Regular practice of TM – for twenty minutes each day, for example – does act as a device to reduce stress and to aid the anticipation of stressful situations which carry crisis potential.

Similar results can be obtained through the practice of systematic relaxation techniques. Here the aim is to totally relax the body and to focus the mind upon the process of relaxation and the feelings that result from such relaxation. In the panel below we outline a short relaxation routine recommended by Stephen Murgatroyd to 26,000 students of the Open University for use just before examinations, which is also valuable before interviews or if important decisions are to be made. To practise the routine it is best to lie on the floor or to sit in a position which helps you feel comfortable. Regular practice of this brief routine each day will also aid in the reduction of stress and increase the ability to cope with stressful situations.

Relaxation Training Exercises

1   Lie down on your back or sit in a chair which supports your back.
2   Close your eyes and try to blot out any sounds. Think only of these instructions.
3   Think about your head. Feel the muscles in your forehead relaxing. Let any creases just drop away. Relax your eyelids. Relax your jaw. Let your tongue fall to the bottom of your mouth. Begin to breathe deeply.
4   Relax your shoulders – let your arms go loose.
5   Relax your neck – let your head roll until you find a comfortable position.
6   Think about your left arm. Tense it and then relax it. Tense it again and relax it slowly. Concentrate on it from the shoulder to the tip of your fingers. Let any tension in the arm flow from your fingers. Let this arm become relaxed.
7   Do the same for your right arm.
8   Think about your left leg from the hip to the knee and from the knee to the tip of your toes. Tense your left leg and then relax it. Tense it harder and then relax it as slowly as you can. Let any tension in this leg flow from your toes. Let this leg become relaxed.
9   Do the same for your right leg.

---

10   Listen now to any sound from within your body – your breathing, your heartbeat, your stomach. Pick one of the sounds and focus on it. Exclude other thoughts from your mind.
11   After about 2–3 minutes slowly open your eyes, sit upright and stretch your arms and legs fully.

Both TM and relaxation training technqiues pay particular attention to the relationship between bodily states and mental states. A considerable amount of the research concerned with stress and crisis points to the importance of body reactions to stressful and crisis events. In particular, muscular tension (back pains, a pain at the base of the neck), severe sweating, indigestion and general feelings of ill health are strongly associated with life-crises. One study by Sydney Cobb, for example, shows that unemployment often acts to exacerbate physical illnesses, especially those related to high levels of body acidity, such as arthritis. The use of techniques which seek to reduce the body-impact of potentially stressful situations may therefore be regarded as anticipatory coping strategies.

Another set of techniques, this time giving emphasis to both the way we think about ourselves and to the way we interact with others, is known as assertiveness. The basic assumption behind this set of coping tactics is that the passive person is most likely to experience stress and crisis because others will take advantage of their passivity and exploit them. Being assertive can therefore help to inhibit crises. Being assertive is not the same as being aggressive. Aggression involves seeking to win in our interactions with others. Being assertive is more concerned with being direct, honest, appropriate, informational, open to further discussion and modification and being responsible. Training in assertiveness skills is often referred to as 'learning to say no without feeling guilty', reflecting the desire to overcome passivity.

Whilst this is a helpful reflection of the purpose of assertiveness training, such training is not restricted to just saying 'no'. It concerns helping individuals assert some simple 'rights'. These rights include the following.

1   The right to change your mind and break commitments which have been made;

2   The right to make mistakes;

3   The right to make decisions or statements without having justifications or even a logical base;

4 The right not to know about something or not to understand;

5 The right to feel and express emotions, both positive and negative, without feeling that it is weak and undesirable to do so;

6 The right not to get involved with someone else's problems or to even feel caring towards them;

7 The right to refuse demands upon you;

8 The right to be the judge of yourself and your own actions and to cope with their consequences;

9 The right to do all of these things listed here without having to justify yourself.

Typical situations in which the quality of assertiveness is valuable in helping to ward off stress are:

(a) when one is blamed for a mistake for which one is not responsible.

(b) when one is asked to undertake a new area of work, despite being already over-burdened and in which the new load is likely to be excessive.

(c) when one is asked to undertake a task within an unrealistic time constraint.

(d) when a person whom we do not like constantly seeks out our company.

(e) when one is asked for a favour over which one has mixed feelings; for example a desire to help a person set against negative feelings likely to be involved in fulfilling the favour.

Three broad tactics are used in assertiveness. First there are *conversation management skills* which aim to encourage effective listening, to enable the person to present his own thoughts, feelings and opinions without feeling that they threaten others and to develop techniques which help others to express themselves. Second there are *reiterative skills*, which enable the person to stay on the point during some sort of confrontation without feeling obliged to apologize, change the subject or withdraw from the interaction. Finally, there are *self-protective skills* which enable the person to stay calm and deal with a verbal attack or anger without feeling personally undermined, devalued or endangered.[1]

All of these skills operate at two levels. First they concern the way the individual thinks about his own position in an interaction with others.

That is why the term 'rights' is used in relation to the nine points listed above. Each of these rights concerns the way the person can be, in an interaction with others.

Second, all of these skills aim at improving the quality of interaction with others in order that potentially stressful or crisis situations can be anticipated and coping strategies negotiated between potential adversaries. It is because assertiveness operates at these two levels that it is here regarded as a form of anticipatory coping.

Transactional analysis, unlike the other forms of anticipatory coping briefly mentioned here, is a 'complete' psychological system. That is to say, transactional analysis – TA for short – offers a description of the psychological development and functioning of a person, irrespective of whether or not that person is experiencing a crisis event. In essence, TA is a conceptual framework for thinking both about self and the interactions a person has with others. It is a language to describe the way a person is. Using TA it is possible to examine and describe interactions between people, or to locate the source of distress or strength in a person's life, and to understand an especially strong response to a particular event. TA is a theoretical and practical tool for understanding a person and the situations he experiences.

It is not our purpose here to offer a complete statement of TA principles and techniques[2]: after all, this is not a book about TA. But one feature of TA is worth elaborating upon at this point. A basic tenet of TA is that the way a person is thinking, feeling and behaving is a function of his "ego-state". Within TA three basic ego-states are described. These are parent (P), adult (A) and child (C).

The parent ego-state is a description of all those behaviours we associate with parenting. On the one hand, these will be supportive and encouraging, seeking to nurture and encourage the development of a person. In contrast, some parenting will be critical, over-protective and demanding. The nurturing parent will use words in their interactions with others like 'try', 'come on now' and 'don't be afraid', whilst the critical parent will use words like 'should', 'if I were you', 'what will other people say' and 'mustn't'. The critical parent will tend to use gestures such as rolling eyes upwards in disgust, tapping feet or wringing hands in impatience, whilst the nurturing parent is most likely to gesture by gentle touches, hugs, winks and encouraging nods. To play at parent does not need the presence of children. The parent ego-state is used in relation to ourselves and in relation to our interactions with others, including wives, friends, workmates, superiors. It is a way of thinking and behaving – just one part of our make-up.

The adult ego-state is another part of our make-up. It involves open, rational and accepting behaviours towards others and ourselves. Typical words and phrases used in adult ego-states are: 'let's think about the problem carefully'; 'let's tackle this together'; 'I am not sure, what do you think?'; 'what are the facts?'; and 'what do you think would be the best thing to do?'. These phrases and words would be spoken calmly and clearly without undue emotion and would be genuine interactions, not part of a 'game'. In a sense, the practice of assertiveness as described above is the practice of the adult ego-state as perceived in transactional analysis.

The final ego-state described within TA is called 'child' and reflects all our experiences and understanding of childhood. In essence, the child ego-state is one in which our actions are determined largely by our feelings and by our needs. The search for recognition ('didn't I do well?' or 'look at me now, aren't I clever?'), for status ('mine's better than yours') and the search for immediate sensation ('gimme', 'I want') are all features of this state.

According to TA, it is possible to characterize our interations with others and our thoughts about ourselves in terms of one or other of these ego-states. We move between them with some regularity. At one moment we will be playing critical parent with ourselves whilst being adult to another person. Later we may shift to being childlike with the other person. These ego-states thus become descriptions of our thoughts about ourselves and of our actions towards others. It is not desirable, according to the founder of TA, Dr Eric Berne, to occupy one state rather than another. The fully functioning person makes use of all three ego-states in his daily life. The person in crisis, however, is often dominated by one or other of these states and finds it difficult to escape from it. The example of Brian might illustrate this clearly.

Brian is forty-three and has been married for twenty years. His wife, Anne, is very adult in her behaviour towards him, rarely showing any child or parent qualities at all. Over the years, Brian has developed a self-critical parent attitude towards himself and this is now beginning to spill-over into his interactions with Anne. Though it is not his intention to be a critical parent towards her, he finds himself forever chastening her for some small things (like the toast being overdone, the flat not being tidy, buying the wrong brand of coffee, wanting to stay in rather than go out, reading too many novels). When he finds himself doing this, he develops a critical parent reaction to himself. In particular, he gets angry with himself and gets angry because he is angry. Within six months, the critical parent reactions to Anne and the critical parent reactions within himself are the only reactions he has and these now cover all aspects of their lives together. Anne persuades him to see a marriage guidance counsellor under the threat of leaving him if he doesn't.

The dominance of one ego-state over all others is the presenting 'cause' of Brian's difficulties. Also involved, though, is the interaction between Anne and Brian, not just in terms of Brian's critical parent behaviour but also in terms of Anne's dominantly adult behaviour and her rare use of the child and parent ego-states. We can show this interaction diagrammatically using the area of some circles to represent the presence/absence of a particular ego-state in both Brian and Anne. The use of such 'ego-grams'

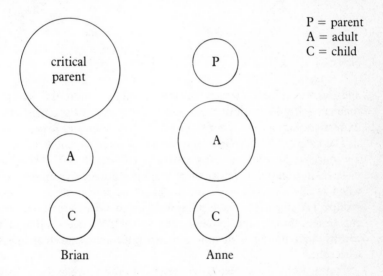

Figure 2.1 Ego-grams of two ego systems at the point of referral to marriage guidance counsellor

in counselling work which uses TA is common. Indeed, in a number of cases, such ego-grams are used throughout the helping process to both describe how a person is and to examine how they would like to be. At the end of four months of one-hour weekly sessions the ego-grams drawn by the counsellor of Brian and Anne looked like this:

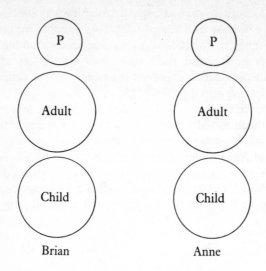

Figure 2.2

and this was achieved largely through an exploration of the ego-states and their meaning for each of them and through the development of a closer understanding of each other's needs between Anne and Brian.

The case of Brian shows, albeit briefly, some potential for the use of TA once a stressful or crisis situation has developed. The reason we include it under the anticipatory coping strategy heading is because, when taught directly to people at school or college or in a community group, TA can help people inhibit or avoid crisis situations because it encourages them to understand more clearly the processes that take place within them and gives them a framework for analysing their interactions with others.

Transactional analysis, assertiveness training, relaxation skills and transcendental meditation are just four tactics representative of the coping strategy labelled 'anticipatory'. Almost all forms of psychological education which aim at improving our understanding of the way we function either in our interaction with others or within ourselves have potential in the framework of anticipatory coping, since they aim to provide us with insights into our past, present and future. As seen from the list of inhibitors to the use of anticipatory coping, insight is a crucial characteristic of the strategy.

The Buffer Strategy

The next strategy to be described by Pearlin and Schooler is the 'buffer' strategy. Put simply, this strategy aims to inhibit the effects upon the person of a stressful or crisis situation, even though the situation itself has developed and does exist. In other words, what is involved here is the re-interpretation of an event so that its effects are perceived as innocuous rather than harmful.

Perhaps the most common buffering tactic is denial, where the person denies to himself or herself the existence of the stressful or crisis situation. For example, those who undergo major surgery often deny to themselves its consequences when these involve reduced physical abilities ('I'll recover in time, no need to hurry'), impaired sexual performance ('it's just a one-off problem') or continuing illness ('it's the drug'). Such denial is also a feature of grief work, as we shall see.

Whilst there must be a doubt about the value of denial when it leads to an ignoring of problems which really should not be ignored, denial can serve useful functions. For example, it can help the person make a more gradual transition from one stage of a situation to another (see Caplan's crisis model in Chapter 1) and can help the person gain time to build up some resistance to the stress and arousal which crisis events cause.

Closely related to denial, but significantly different from it, is *repression*. Repression means that a person experiencing some crisis or stressful life-event chooses to ignore selectively certain aspects of that situation (e.g., the feelings or fears that he or she has) in order that they might simply live through it. One effective technique used by those who wish to repress the undesirable consequences of their situation is selective ignoring which leads the individual to 'select out' some positive feature of the experience and focus his thoughts upon this to the exclusion of all others. For example, a rape victim coped with her experience for a considerable period of time by telling herself that the chances of her being raped again were almost zero. Many people cope with aspects of grief relating to the death of a person who had a terminal illness by telling themselves that at least the suffering is over. Similarly, the parents of a daughter killed in a tragic car accident repressed a great many of their feelings by telling themselves that her death was instantaneous. Where repression differs from denial is that the person accepts that he is experiencing some form of crisis or stressful life-event; he then represses many of its consequences and, in doing so, buffers himself from the full range of these experiences.

A further form of buffering is *reaction-formation*. Whilst this sounds complicated, it is in fact a very simple idea. Essentially it involves people doing the opposite of what they think and feel, but doing it unconsciously so that they begin to allow their behaviour to determine their thoughts and feelings. For example, people in grief often obsessively bury themselves in work and begin to believe that they have managed their grief because they are working so hard. This obsessive enthusiasm for work is often an indication of incomplete grief work.

Perhaps the most elaborate forms of reaction-formation occur in reaction to sexual difficulties. Here the person reacts by zealous campaigns against sexual behaviours of various kinds and by a desire to remove pornography or sexual deviation from his or her world. Such obsessional campaigning behaviour may well mask an unconscious desire for sexual gratification and for deviant sex. Clearly, reaction-formation is not a description of everyone who campaigns against sexual deviation or pornography. But for those who seek to displace their strong desires – to buffer themselves against their own feelings which they find difficult to control – campaigning against sexual displays, for example, permits them both to appear virtuous and to wallow in the displays themselves.

The final tactic we shall describe here of buffer coping is called *positive comparison*. Here the stressful and crisis nature of a current event is compared favourably with the stressful or crisis nature of some previous event or the response to a similar situation of another person. For example, hospital patients in orthopaedic surgery wards often compare themselves with other patients on the ward who have lost more limbs than they have – saying 'well at least I've got more legs than he has'. Unemployed persons in the 1980s often compare themselves favourably with their grandparents who were unemployed in the 1930s – 'at least we have supplementary benefits and the dole!'

All of these tactics can have short-term benefits. They permit the person to cope with the immediate feelings and thoughts that pertain to the crisis-event. But all are weak as long-term tactics, since they do not provide a means either of developing anticipatory coping skills or of working through the underlying emotions, thoughts and actions in such a way as to permit transition learning to occur. For example, if a person who has experienced the loss of a husband or wife initially denies the loss, this may help him to cope with its most immediate effects. If the person continues to deny, then he will fail to work through the stages of grief and may have difficulty in coping either with his own fears about his own death, with the death of others close to him, or with making relationships intended to replace or substitute for the dead person.[3] Whilst valuable at one level, the buffer strategy can, as we have seen, have severe limitations.

The Crisis-Management Strategy

The characteristic feature of this strategy, which contrasts sharply with the characteristics of the other strategies, is that the person changes neither the situation which is giving rise to a crisis experience nor himself. He simply finds effective ways of dealing with the effects of the situation. That is, he aims to ease the discomfort of experiences in a crisis rather than to avoid the crisis (anticipatory strategy) or to deny its consequences (buffer strategy). Put simply, crisis-management is best regarded as reactive.

Whereas the identification of particular tactics was possible with the coping strategies described above, the crisis-management strategy makes use of any tactic provided that it seems likely significantly to affect the experience of distress and reduce the level of tension. Relaxation training or positive comparison may all be used as tactics within this strategy. We may also refer to *cognitive restructuring* under this heading. The aim here is to take a catastrophizing thought or feeling and to de-objectify if, by moving it into the here and now. So, for example, a painful situation which involves feelings such as 'Oh my God I'm going to lose all control' can be reconceptualized as something like 'this may be painful and upsetting but I've coped with difficult situations in the past and I don't have to go to pieces over this'. By inserting the three words 'right now I' before a painful thought or feeling, an alternative reformulation can be encouraged – e.g., 'This will never end' becomes 'Right now I feel pain, but deep down I know that things can only get better.' Such a reformulation helps to elevate the emotional content behind each statement out of its reified, objectified state as something external to and disowned by the individual. It encourages him also to disentangle past, present and future; to get in touch with feelings in the 'here and now'; to acknowledge the links between cognitive and affective states; and to accept responsibility for his own thoughts and feelings.

This discussion leads to an important realization. The strategy a person adopts acts to determine the way in which specific tactics are used. To some extent, then, tactics are independent of strategy: the two interact only to determine the specific use of a tactic.

In later sections of this book we shall be documenting in detail the tactics that may be helpful in particular situations and describing in detail the helping process appropriate to different kinds of helping. The key point to note here is that the person's coping strategy will determine both the selection of tactics and the precise way in which they are used. It is essential, therefore, that attempts to promote coping pay close attention to the coping strategy a person adopts and the motives which have led that person to adopt that strategy.

There is good evidence that coping developed in one context (e.g., divorce) helps the person to become equipped for future situations (e.g., bereavement, unemployment). One task which helpers can usefully be engaged in is the active promotion of the transfer of coping skills by: (a) increasing the repertoire of coping tactics available to the person; and (b) making explicit the transferable nature of each tactic.

Individuals find new tactics for coping with life-stress and crisis. Not all of these coping tactics will be documented in a book of this kind. The fact that a particular method of coping is not included here or later should not be taken to imply that it is not effective or valuable. If it works it is! Rather, the intention of this book is to provide some tools for critical self-reflection on the nature of coping and the value of particular coping tactics. Later chapters seek to outline some tactics which might be usefully added to a person's repertoire. In discussion of particular crisis problems, such tactics will also be documented.

1. If you would like to know more about these skills, see Smith, Manuel J. (1975): *When I Say No, I Feel Guilty*. New York. Dial Press.
2. See Harris, Thomas A. (1973): *I'm OK – You're OK*. Pan: London.
3. For a discussion of the value of externalizing stress through mechanisms like projection and displacement see Haan C. (1977): *Coping and Defending: processes of self-environment organization*. New York: Academic Press.

PART TWO: CRISES

3 Change and Development in Adult Life – A Context for Crisis

4 Divorce and Separation

5 Being Young in an Old Community – Adolescence and Crisis

6 Growing Old or Older and Growing – Crisis and Old Age

7 Parenting and Handicap – Acceptance of the Unacceptable

8 Unemployment – the Person and the Family

9 Loss and Grief

10 Rape

CHAPTER 3

CHANGE AND DEVELOPMENT IN ADULT LIFE – A CONTEXT FOR CRISES

Introduction

At first sight, this may seem an unusual chapter for a book whose primary focus is upon specific crises, such as divorce, rape, death and loss, unemployment and ageing. Adulthood seems a rather normal and stable state, most unlike the kind of crisis events listed here. But there are good grounds for seeing adult life as a period in which significant changes do occur – changes which may place the individual in transitional or crisis situations.

These changes are not simply questions of biological maturation. They also concern the models or stereotypes of being 'an adult' in our society. For these models influence the way in which individuals learn to perceive and understand their own circumstances and reactions. The very nature of adult life involves biological and social change; coping with these changes is not just a marginal but a central feature of adult life for all individuals. These changes have to be managed in a social context and the view that others have of the changes and developments that occur in a person's life can affect the success of a person's coping strategy and can impair or enhance his developing maturity.

Terms like 'mid-life crisis' have now become part of our daily linguistic currency. They are accepted as if they were both generally true and adequately descriptive of a particular process. But these terms are just generalized statements about the experience of adulthood. In our view, understanding normal and developmental changes that occur in adulthood is an essential prerequisite for understanding crisis experiences. Looking at developmental changes helps us to recognize that crises take place not in a static context but in the context of a naturally changing and evolving person.

Barrie Hopson and Mike Scally of the University of Leeds make a distinction between 'change' and 'development'. While change offers a potential for development, it is not a sufficient condition for development to take place. It is possible for a person to change in a way that inhibits or prevents development. As these two writers make clear, 'for a change to be developmental there needs to be a movement towards a greater realization of personal potential, i.e., acquiring new skills, increasing self- awareness, and clarifying one's values. Our operational definition of development involves the person being more "self-empowered", i.e., more proactive, less dependent upon others, valuing the integrity of others as well as themselves, more in charge of themselves and their lives' (Hopson and Scally, 1980). In short, these writers suggest that the person is developing only when the changes he experiences lead to enhanced coping and self-direction. They also suggest that helpers have an important role in helping the changing person towards development by encouraging him to examine the stereotypes of adulthood and ageing which he uses to inform his thinking and by encouraging him to be more self- disclosing. Through this kind of help the person can be freed from many of the self-imposed constraints which inhibit his development and become more self-directing and autonomous as an individual.

Kinds of Change

In writing about change and development in adult life, many sociologists and psychologists employ a variety of different concepts. The idea of stages figures prominently in the pioneering work of Erik Erikson (Erikson, 1950). Erikson saw individuals as being faced with a series of 'personal crises' or turning points throughout their lives. The successful resolution of each crisis is necessary for the person to be able to face and cope with the next. Erikson suggests that there are three adult stages, which are themselves crisis-laden. The first is concerned with the person's need to establish intimate relationships. To form such relationships, the person has to fuse his own identity with that of others, through marrige or other stable relationships. These relationships, once established, give rise to a further need, which Erikson regards as the need to give of oneself to others through, for example, community service and mutual aid. Erikson suggests that if this need to give of oneself to others does not arise then the person stagnates and becomes self-centred in such a way as to inhibit his development and make coping with particular crisis events more difficult to achieve. The final stage suggested by Erikson concerns the view of the meaning of his life which a person has towards old age. Erikson would perceive mid-life crisis as occuring when a person feels that he or she has lost a sense of purpose, while emotional problems in old age may arise as a result of the individual seeing his life as a series of missed opportunities and failures. Successful passage through these stages, Erikson implies, leads to feelings of fulfilment, purposiveness and to an enhanced ability to cope with the biological features of ageing.

Erikson is not the only person to suggest these stages. Others suggest that there are stages related directly to key concerns of a particular period of life. Havighurst, an American who has studied adult development, suggests that the passages a person moves through primarily concern his relationship to work. In early adulthood the concern is to establish an identity in relation to others through work. As he becomes older and more established at work he seeks to consolidate his personal relationships. As he nears retirement he begins to seek to understand more of himself and to establish what he wishes to happen to him in the future. Though the focus of these stages is rather different from those suggested by Erikson, both models have one thing in common. It is that before a person can reach a stage he must resolve for himself (and in his own way) the dilemmas and difficulties of the previous stage. Working through these stages is essential for development – such work (similar to the work of worry, see pages 105 to 119) is a necessary developmental task.

Given these kinds of stages and the necessity for each to be worked through in some way before it is possible for the next stage to be reached, crises are not unusual events. Rather, they are to be expected as a normal feature of adult life. Whilst some crises are not a part of this developmental model – rape, divorce and unemployment are rarely experienced directly by the majority of adults – crises will occur and will lead to either development or stagnation (Gould, 1978; Levinson, 1978).

Whilst the idea of adult life involving stages is attractive – it helps us understand a series of complex processes – it is simplistic. First, not everyone passes through all of these stages. Many get 'stuck' at various points. Secondly, it is not possible to provide a description of all the variants on each of these stages since each variant will relate more to the unique experiences of a particular person. Third, some people have such successful coping tactics that they experience these stages as a smooth, uninterrupted flow. Finally, there is a danger that these stages will be associated with particular age periods. The enormously popular book

Passages is subtitled *Predictable crises of adult life* and uses terms like 'the trying twenties', the 'catch thirties' and 'the forlorn forties' – all of which imply that the individual is locked into an inevitable cycle tied to his chronological age.

The idea of stages for development is useful if used sensitively. Stages should not be regarded as either definitive statements about the course of an adult's life or as models for the work of a helper. They are more like reference points on a map that may occasionally help a person review the direction of their lives. Recent research carried out in Britain shows clearly that 'we are by no means slaves to our age, as the simple theory of the adult human life-cycle would have us believe. Most people, far from being obsessed by how old they happen to be, are quite surprised by the suggestion that their personality, behaviour or feelings have anything to do with their age' (Nicholson, 1980). This research provides us with much more grounds for optimism about the natural development of the adult. As Nicholson, the key reseracher, puts it: 'when we do change in adulthood, it is not as a result simply of the passage of time, but rather because of major life-events, many (though not all) of which we wish upon ourselves.' Amongst these critical life-events we might include leaving the parental home, getting married, changing a job, having a child, getting a divorce, moving house, having a mistress or boyfriend. None of these are inevitable. All involve some element of choice. Once this choice element is acknowledged, it becomes possible for helpers to recognize their role in preventing crises (through enabling the person to develop anticipatory coping and encouraging him to make more informed decisions and to become more self-aware) as well as in helping him cope with the consequences of crises.

The Life Course

Rather than speak of the 'adult life-cycle' or 'passages' we shall use the term 'life-course', also used by Ken Giles and Ray Woolfe in their work for the Open University (Giles and Woolfe, 1981). It is more neutral than either of the other terms and is not as tied to notions of age or work.

The life-course involves a number of key concerns for a person. Sometimes this course will move through various issues that confront him as if age was a key variable. At other times and for other people, the issue becomes of importance irrespective of the age a person has achieved. The following issues are dominant in the normal life-course documented by many writers, most notably Huberman (1974):

1 *Focusing one's life* – establishing a coherent identity through work, marriage, social relationships and community involvement. Though this is often associated with young adulthood, it is clear that adults of all ages return to this issue from time to time and seek to re-establish their focus.

2 *Collecting one's energies* – a relatively stable period in which the person engages in a considerable amount of activity with others, often finding himself in the role of helper or befriender.

3 *Exerting and assuring oneself* – an active interest is taken in the world of work, politics and current affairs; children leave home and those who had been house-parents consider returning to work; the focus here is very much upon the person's place in the community and the impact of that community upon that person.

4 *Maintaining position and changing roles* – the person begins to focus upon his 'self' much more and addresses himself to his own needs, especially short-term and immediate needs.

5 *Deciding whether and how to disengage* – the person becomes more withdrawn from his community and society and focuses primarily upon himself; there is a striving towards the meeting of emotional and physical needs and a period of seeking to rationalise his relationship with others, almost as if he were seeking a firm contractual basis for his relationship.

6 *Making the most of disengagement* – whilst he remains self-focused, he nonetheless recognizes his dependence upon others and seeks to maximize the benefits he obtains from such relationships. This is a very characteristic period of old age in particular, though it is not exclusively tied to being elderly.

The idea of this model is that an individual will, from time to time, find himself dominantly concerned with one of these six areas. Some will pass through the six as if there were a natural progression from one to another; others will get stuck at one or other; yet others will seek to disengage from the process of the life-course completely for a time, returning to it later. The model gives a flavour of the life-course – more map reference points – it is not intended to be presented as though of self evident validity.

Many helpers have sought to encourage individuals to work through some of the issues raised in the model. In particular, adult educators of all kinds have invested time and energy in work intended to minimize crisis and maximize the possibility of development. Huberman identifies three objectives which these educators have actively pursued:

(a) *helping adults cope with the increased pace of social change* – in particular, helping them examine their role in relation to their family, religion and the state and to develop coping skills appropriate for the rapidly changing worlds of work, leisure and non-work;

(b) *helping adults to continue their learning so that they can adjust to new situations and learn new skills* – this includes work on job-skills, preparation for retirement, self-development and personal growth, artistic and musical skills and many others;

(c) *helping the person fill adult roles and meet adult responsibilities* – this includes education for vocational competence, parent education, consumer and health education and asserting citizens' rights.

All these concerns are typical of the programmes of many educational establishments, churches, friendly society's and self-help groups. They suggest that adults need to be formally prepared for their roles in the community and for the changes they are to experience. But investment in adult educational resources and opportunities is minimal. The major educational investments in most of the developed world are in educational systems which seek to prepare young people for their roles as workers. Few countries have developed educational systems in which adults are regarded as needing educational resources to help them cope with the significant changes they will experience. Indeed, in many countries the provision of appropriate adult education is left to chance. One role for helpers, over and above helping the individual cope with his own changes and developments (not to mention crises), involves them helping individuals initiate social change so that more resources will be devoted to the educational and personal needs of adults.

Some Development Tasks for Helpers

The point being made here is that helpers, to be effective, need to do more than simply work with individuals. For example, the helper who works simply with unemployed people as individuals is unlikely to be helping them organize effective political action to secure policies which will lead to the creation of more jobs. The helper who laments the lack of developmental educational resources but does nothing to mobilize such resources is unlikely to secure these resources. Whilst not all helpers will wish to engage the social system in this way, the 'helper as advocate' is an important role, too often neglected in the study of crisis, change and development.

In addition to their role as advocates, helpers have two other major roles to perform in the context of normal adult development. The first is, to borrow a phrase from Mezirow (1977), 'perspective transformation' – meaning helping the person change and transform his taken-for-granted assumptions about himself, his relationships in the social world, his relationships with others and his future. Helpers need to encourage the person to be able to 'become critically aware of the cultural and psychological assumptions that influence the way we see ourselves . . . our relationships and the way we pattern our lives'. Essentially, this task involves helpers in encouraging critical self-reflection. In pursuing this task it is important to recognize that the person doing the reflecting is the one that should determine the direction in which the reflection is going. The helper's task is not to direct but to facilitate self-direction.

A second task for helpers is to help the person recognize the way in which the assumptions others make about him affect his attitudes, thoughts, feelings and actions. To increase a person's ability to look at the expectations of others, at the way in which social conditions shape his choices and actions and to enable him to see ways in which he can achieve his ambitions and meet his needs within the framework of existing social conditions – all these are important helping objectives. Sometimes the helper will need to go further and help the person recognize that the achievement of certain of his own ambitions or fulfillment of his needs will be consequent upon some change in the views or behaviour of others.

Conclusion

This brief chapter seeks to suggest two things. First, crisis events are a normal feature of adulthood. Whilst some of the crises documented in this text are unlikely to be common, it is important to recognize that normal adult development involves the person developing through his experience of difficult and crisis-laden events. Second, the helper's task is not restricted to working on a person with 'problems' – normal development is significantly aided by helpers. Associated with this observation is the suggestion that helpers need to focus upon their role as advocates as well as their role as facilitators.

Later chapters in this book will look at adolescent development and ageing in the context of developmental stages and the life-course. The purpose of this chapter is to set the context for those chapters dealing with more specific crisis experiences.

CHAPTER 4

DIVORCE AND SEPARATION

Divorce is a growing feature of many societies. In Britain, current divorce rates and estimations of the number of separations suggest that one in three married couples can be expected to be involved in either divorce or separation. The same figure for the United States is one in two. Divorce and separation and related distresses are thus a common source of crisis for families, whether or not children are involved.

In this chapter we shall examine the causes of divorce, the divorcing process and the consequences of divorce, using case materials throughout to illustrate the nature of the thoughts, feelings and behaviours typically documented in studies of divorcing couples and their families. In addition, we shall seek to identify the roles that can be played by those wishing to help divorcing couples or separated persons and their children. This chapter has been written following our own experience of working with divorcing and divorced persons and is related to a review of the substantial literature dealing with divorce, some of which will be described in this chapter for those wishing to gain further insights and understanding of the divorce process and its consequences.

Reasons for Divorce and the Divorce-Unfolding Process

There are many reasons for divorce. Some are triggered by a particular event, such as a sudden change in the financial status of the family following a 'poor' decision by one of the marriage partners. Others are the inevitable consequences of a lack of understanding of the implications of marriage or of a failure to know the marriage partner well enough before marriage. Occasionally a marriage ends because of the failure of one partner to satisfy the other sexually. The most common reasons for divorce are:

physical violence triggered by a variety of events

a growing failure to communicate thoughts and feelings, except in relation to trivial matters;

an absence of respect, acceptance or 'love' between the partners;

fundamental differences of personality which are irrecoverable;

a gradual growing apart;

sexual unfaithfulness – breaking with the assumption of fidelity.

For a large number of cases, according to studies by Kenneth Kressel and others, separation and divorce occur because 'wives wanted a more intimate, emotionally closer relationship than their husbands were willing or able to supply'.

Some couples, in exploring their feelings about becoming separated or getting divorced, find that all the conditions listed above apply to them in some degree. Others are not able to be as specific as this list may imply: they just feel divorce or separation is a valid response to their 'problem'.

In all cases, the decision to seek a divorce or to separate is the result of a period during which the issues have unfolded as prime concerns for the couple. During this unfolding process many different types of reactions, thoughts, feelings and behaviours may occur. The unfolding period lasts between one and thirty months and is usually ended by one of the partners taking action such as moving out or initiating divorce proceedings.

Kenneth Kressel and his co-workers in New York, already mentioned above, have produced a set of descriptions of different types of couples engaged in the unfolding process. These different types depend upon the strength of three sets of thoughts and feelings. These are: (a) the extent to which the couple is ambivalent towards the fate of the relationship – do they really care about whether they stay married or not?; (b) the frequency and openers of communications concerning the possibility of divorce – do they really talk about their thoughts and feelings towards each other?; and (c) the extent to which they are openly in conflict with each other. Using these three sets of thoughts and feelings, Kressel has identified four types of divorcing couples. Each of these is described briefly below.

First there is the type of couple who can be said to be *enmeshed*. They are openly in conflict, frequently and heatedly communicating their thoughts and feelings about each other to each other, and they are highly ambivalent about the future of their marriage. Most commonly this type of couple verbalize their decision to divorce but find themselves physically and emotionally incapable of separation. The case of the Lewals illustrates this type.

Stan and Betty Lewal are both twenty-seven and have been married for three years. Apart from the first eight months of their marriage, when their relationship was healthy, the couple have argued violently about their relationship, about the respective failure of each other to work at being married and about alleged unfaithfulness. Gradually they have grown more and more apart and come together only to argue or to agree to separate. Yet on each occasion they have decided to separate (sometimes after a period in marriage guidance) no physical steps have been taken. Throughout their marriage they have continued to sleep with each other and (surprisingly) have continued to have a close sexual relationship – it seems as if they were physically unable to let go of each other.

As is clear from this brief description, the enmeshed type are attached to each other at a number of levels not easily identifiable. It is also difficult for them and for others seeking to help them (friends and marriage guidance counsellors) to penetrate their arguments so as to get at the features which are really holding them together.

A second type of divorcing couple are best thought of as *autistic*. For this type, communication of thoughts and feelings concerning their partner are notable by their absence and conflict is not apparent. Ambivalence is high, but is sublimated by the need to avoid conflict and by continuing, surging currents of doubts and uncertainty which are rarely (if at all) articulated. Indeed, the relationships between such couples are best thought of in terms of avoidance: avoidance of thoughts, feelings, actions, which may upset either the partner, themselves or both. The Cornas are a typical example of the autistic type.

Mike and Mary Corna are thirty-two and thirty-four respectively and have been married eleven years. They have a son aged nine. Mike travels as a part of his work and in the period immediately preceding the decision to separate he was required by his company to work in a city some two hundred miles from his home. They decided that it is best for him to live in this city during the week and to travel home at weekends. During this period away, Mike decided to divorce Mary, but did not communicate this decision to Mary until a month after his return to full-time residence with the family. Mary demurely accepted this decision, saying that they were growing more and more distant anyway and if that is what he felt best for him then she would accept. There was practically no discussion of either the reasons for divorce or the consequences – lawyers settled the terms of the divorce between themselves. In a discussion with a friend the wife blamed the divorce on years of non-communication and their mutual fear of upsetting each other.

For the Cornas, avoidance of feelings and the repression of thoughts that might arouse feelings were key features of their coping behaviour prior to and during the unfolding period.

A third type of divorcing couple are regarded as being in *direct conflict*. Though they are openly in conflict with each other the conflict is not as embittered as in the case of the enmeshed couple and they frequently discuss their feelings towards each other and their thought about the future of their relationship; the key to an understanding of this type of couple is their diminishing ambivalence. At the beginning of the unfolding process they appear to be highly ambivalent about the separation, but as the unfolding continues they become increasingly convinced that separation represents the only realistic outcome for them. What appears to happen in this relationship is that the unfolding process gradually weakens the feelings of guilt, sense of failure, tension and fears about separation associated with the decision to divorce, thus making the decision increasingly likely. The Zorza family are an especially clear illustration of this type.

Ludmilla and Sven Zorza, aged twenty-two and thirty respectively, had been discussing divorce for six and a half months. Though they had many heated and protracted discussions, they were unable to resolve the issue. To provide a basis for helping them resolve their ambivalence they attended a family therapy centre for four one-hour sessions. Though a therapeutic contact of only four hours is brief, its effects were catalytic. Sven felt that the degree of empathy shown towards them by their counsellor was such that it showed him that they were right to be asking about divorce; it also showed that other people accepted divorce as a possible solution to marital failure and this in turn acted to reduce his feelings of guilt and anxiety. He wanted a divorce. If Sven's reactions to brief therapy seem to mark a dramatic change from being indecisive to being decisive, Ludmilla's reaction is even more dramatic. She agreed with Sven that divorce was inevitable, that she shouldn't and wouldn't feel guilty and in no way was divorce a sign of personal failure. She moved out of their home and lived with a female friend who had divorced some two and a half years previously, using the friend as a model for successful coping.

The ease of this separation was not matched, however, by the legal settlement. Both have made three court appearances in attempts to reverse decisions made at the time of the original legal settlement. Though living apart and legally divorced, they remain in direct conflict.

This case provides a vivid illustration not only of the direct conflict type but also of the fact that conflict does not end with the separation and divorce settlement – a point we shall return to below.

The final type identified in studies of divorcing couples is referred to as the *disengaged type*. This type are not in conflict, rarely communicate their thoughts and feelings about each other to each other and are clearly determined to separate. The process of unfolding begins with the decision to divorce, thus reducing the degree of conflict and the need for communication. As one writer expresses this, 'of all other couples, these were the ones in which the flame of intimacy had come to burn least brightly – and so too the heat of conflict' (Kendall et al., 1980). The Saunders couple provide a case illustration of this type.

Sandra and William Saunders, both aged forty-three, had a daughter aged twelve and a son aged sixteen. They decided on a trial separation after a very brief discussion of the fact that they had, over the years, just drifted apart. The trial separation was seen as an important 'cooling off period' and one in which either reconciliation or separation were seen as possible outcomes. After the agreed six months period of trial separation the couple came back together for six days during which they explored the outcome of the trial through brief, non-emotional and sporadic conversations. These conversations were characterized by low levels of disclosure of thoughts and feelings. Both felt, they said, that they no longer had enough in common with each other to justify marriage – both seemed to have lost interest in each other and in the idea of reconciliation. They separated, were formally divorced and see each other briefly at birthdays and Christmas. Whilst these post-divorce meetings are tense, both continue to feel that they did the right thing and that their children are not affected by their estrangement.

These four types of divorcing couples do not constitute an exhaustive statement of either the unfolding process or the experience of divorce. Clearly, there are many hybrids of these types and there may well be many different types not documented here. But even this typology enables us to make three observations in line with major themes of this book. First, divorce is the end product of a complex process with many facets. No two divorcing or separating couples will have the same characteristic experiences, feelings or thoughts. These types are reference points to help clarify the nature of the thoughts, feelings and actions engaged by a particular couple. Second, these different types suggest different forms of coping. Some cope with their divorce decision by letting out anger whilst others repress or deny this feeling. Others resolve feelings of guilt by making a firm, shared decision to separate whilst some remain guilty afterwards. Couples cope differently with divorce. Finally, these types show the complex inter-relationships between thoughts, feelings and action. The Lewel case makes this point abundantly clear: a resolution at a rational level to act does not necessarily lead to action. Divorce, like other forms of personal crisis, can affect all levels of individual functioning.

Settlement Issues in Divorce and Separation – Structured Mediation

Before examining the consequences of divorce and separation for the well-being of all those affected and before examining the constructive role that can be played by helpers wishing to help one or other of the former partners or their children, some attention needs to be given to the practical issues to which divorce gives rise.

The decision to divorce or separate has some very direct consequences. Often, couples and families do not fully appreciate the range and extent of some of these changes, and need help in formulating an agenda for change so as to rationally examine consequences.

O. J. Coogler, a lawyer and psychotherapist, has suggested that the majority of divorcing couples need direct assistance in the mediation of the practical consequences of divorce. In particular mediation which helps them settle such issues as:

who shall have custody of the children?

what rights should the non-custodial parent have in relation to visits to the children?

what contact, if any, is to take place between the couple after the divorce?

what financial support should be made available to the children of the marriage and how should this support be provided?

what financial arrangements should exist between the divorcing couple (the question of alimony)?

how should the couple's property and goods be divided?

Such mediation is thought of not only in terms of settlement but also as a constructive and real focus for helping the couple face up to and cope with their separation.

The programme of structured mediation described by Coogler in his book *Structured Mediation in Divorce Settlement* constitutes a framework within which couples can directly negotiate on each of the above issues. A mediator acts as a facilitator of these negotiations by providing direct assistance with deciding on an agenda, developing the problem-solving skills of the participants, increasing the flow of accurate, helpful and non-beligerant information, and ensuring that both parties participate actively in the design of a mutually acceptable divorce settlement. In addition, the mediator seeks to establish firm ground rules for the structured mediation. These include: (a) no use of lawyers by either couple, other than the one neutral lawyer recommended by the mediator; (b) emotional and adjustment problems are referred elsewhere – they have no place in the structured mediation; (c) the requirement of full disclosure of thoughts, feelings and intended actions on the above questions; (d) the need for fairness and mutual respect in the conduct of the mediation. The mediator seeks to ensure that these ground rules are followed throughout the mediation process. To aid them, mediators generally begin by obtaining a written agreement to adhere to these rules – this agreement forms the basis of a helping contract. It also helps the mediator avoid dealing with emotional problems, which are always referred elsewhere.

As an alternative to lawyers arguing between themselves at the expense of the divorcing couple, this mediation process holds considerable promise. But there is some evidence that it does not work well with all types of couples. Returning to the four types described above, this form of structured mediation works well with the direct and disengaged types but not as well with the autistic and enmeshed types. For these two types, for different reasons, resist settlement and appear to feel cheated, whatever the outcomes. It is interesting to note too that some early research studies indicate a higher degree of post-divorce coping failure amongst the enmeshed and autistic types.

We briefly describe the process of structured mediation and the issues it seeks to resolve for two reasons. First, not all consequences of divorce and separation are emotional – some are practical. It is just as important to examine these and the ways that have been developed to resolve these issues as it is to examine the emotional consequences. Practical and emotional consequences can both give rise to crisis experiences. Second, the brief description of structured mediation provided here is a description of a role that can be played by a netural friend or helper. Indeed, it may be a useful role for the neutral helper in a marriage guidance or community advice agency to play, especially given the opportunity it provides to refer the couple to others if more help is needed in the area of emotional adjustment.

Emotional Consequences of Divorce and Separation

The list of items to be discussed in a divorce settlement involving children, given above, makes it clear that divorce and separation involve loss. For the parent who does not gain custody of his or her child, the losses could involve the loss of home, of children, of some friends, of certain possessions, of some income, of status and the loss of a fantasy – the fantasy of a stable life uninterrupted by crisis. For others, it may involve a loss of dependence, of security or of outlets for sexual release. Reactions to divorce by the adults involved and by their children are many and varied. In this section we are not able to examine all possible reactions to divorce. Instead we focus upon the major patterns of reactions and their consequences.

A commonly reported reaction to separation and divorce amongst many couples is one of continued feelings of attachment to the former spouse. Weiss, in a book called *Marital Separation*, suggests that these feelings of continued attachment are 'almost universal'. In two cases in which we were involved, the former marriage partners met regularly on a given day of the week and occasionally engaged in sexual relations. In many other cases, the former spouse is regarded as a 'best friend'. Whilst not all who have a continued feeling of attachment act upon this feeling it is nonetheless common.

Also common amongst the reported changes resulting from divorce are the following:

a change in life-style (forced by changes in income status) and a change in life-pattern (forced by loss of partner), leading to a challenge to the person's identity;

a change in a person's way of relating to children, the change being different for the custodial and non-custodial parent;

a change in the nature and frequency of relationships with other adults;

a change in the sexual life of the person;

a change in the number and frequency of tedious duties that need to be performed – tasks formerly shared (washing-up, ironing, gardening, decorating, planning, shopping, house-repairs) have now to be done alone;

a change in the frequency with which it is possible to share intimate thoughts, feelings and concerns.

For the children of divorcing couples, there are other changes, though these are experienced differently by children of different ages as we shall see. They include:

a new kind of relationship with their non-custodial parent;

changes in their relationship with their custodial parent and further adjustments to their new life-style, especially if this parent seeks relief from being a single-parent through new courtships;

changes in housing arrangements and income status may lead to changes in schools which in turn involve the loss of friends and stability;

in the case of young children where the custodial parent needs to work, there may be an increased attendance at play groups or nursery school, with associated adjustment needs.

Not all of the consequences of divorce and separation are negative. As Dlugokinski* reminds us, divorce and separation represent the 'ending of a self-defeating relationship'. The act of separation serves to reduce specific conflict, ends a period of uncertainty and reduces the need to guard against certain kinds of communication which may offend or lead to recrimination. Separation has a number of other liberating features. The person is free to engage in eccentricities without fear of the reactions of others. This has led some to eat fish and chips in bed, to stay up all night reading, to watch television programmes previously denied to them and to prepare the same meal on six consecutive nights just because they wanted to! The fact of separation removes the need to be concerned about the reactions of others to sexual exploration and has led some to explore more fully their own sexuality. Fear of the other spouse and anger at the marital relationship is ended.

For the children of divorced or separated couples, the liberating effects are also apparent. Because they now have one parent and not two, they sometimes feel that they are given more attention and that a new improved bonding is taking place with the custodial parent. Often too, their relationship with the non-custodial parent changes, becoming more intense and generous. No longer do they feel they are being used as pawns in an attempt to hold together a marriage, but now they are being more genuinely respected. Finally, they have new responsibilities – older children especially begin to feel that they are conjointly responsible for the new single-parent household.

Whether positive or negative, these consequences of divorce all involve change – some of it significant, challenging and crisis-laden. Those involved have to discover ways of coping with these changes – this being made more difficult by the variety and frequency of the changes themselves.

To help us understand reactions to separation following divorce and to view the coping strategies and tactics typically employed, a three-stage coping model is here described. The stages are: (a) *orientation* – the stage at which the full range of consequences is realized; (b) *integration* – the stage at which coping strategies to deal with consequences are developed; and (c) *consolidation* – the stage at which the coping strategies lead to permanent adaptation and change in the way the divorced person thinks, feels and behaves. In the detailed descriptions which follow the meaning of each of these stages will be documented and illustrated with case studies and tasks for helpers will be identified. A subsequent section of this chapter will examine in detail the reactions of children.

Stage 1: Orientation

During this period the person has to cope with a large number of new situations and significant changes in others. Often individuals are overloaded by these changes and experience high stress and tension. To cope with the new demands being made upon them, they typically: (a) deny that divorce is leading them to change their thoughts, feelings or behaviours in any significant way; (b) react to their stress by feeling depressed or becoming helpless; (c) seek refuge in some outlet, such as drinking, drugs (doctor prescribed or otherwise) or frequent sexual encounters. At this stage, individuals cope either in adaptive or maladaptive ways. Though denial is likely to be a feature of the phase, adaptive responses seek to minimize stress without denying that it is present; maladaptive responses seek to obliterate stress and deny the sources of its origin.

The task of the person seeking to help at this stage involves three components. First, there is a need to encourage accurate understanding. This involves isolating the specific sources of stress and distress and the thoughts, feelings and behaviours associated with them. Check-lists and self-contracts (Chapter 11 may be a valuable aid in this process). Second, the person needs a model of self-care and respect. Helpers need to demonstrate in direct ways their care and concern and to show respect for the person whilst at the same time being active in their pursuit of accurate understanding. Helpers should not assume that their care and concern, once evidenced, need not be directly a focus for discussion: occasional, but forceful reminders of the concern and respect felt by helpers serve both to encourage the person in distress and provide a model for the direct expression of feeling. Finally, there is a need to ensure that the work of the helper does not become a part of the person's problem rather than a part of the 'solution'. Unreal expectations of the outcomes of helping can have many stressful consequences. The helper needs an explicit contract with the person which acknowledges both the skills of the helper and the needs of the person. This contract needs to be reviewed and renewed from time to time but needs to be regarded as a firm basis for the helping relationship. We shall say more about such contracts and their form a little later in this book (see Chapter 11).

Stage 2: Integration

Whereas the previous stage is characterized by the attempt to work through the issues, feelings and responses to problems created by the separation and by the attempt to establish a particular identity this stage is characterized by a balanced view of the situation. In short, there is a growing awareness of the specific advantages and disadvantages of separation and a realization that the changes involved constitute a need to redefine identity. 'Who am I' is the key question in this period of intensive worry work.

Two maladaptive coping strategies are sometimes adopted at this stage. These are: (a) *repression* – used as a means of avoiding anxiety; (b) *depression* – used as a response to anxiety. In both these responses, guilt and resentment become characteristic thoughts and hopelessness and bitterness characteristic feelings.

Adaptive responses involve the attempt to experience and work through the emotions and thoughts in such a way as to seek both to control them and to put them to use in the construction of an identity. 'Mastery not misery' is the essential aim of adaptive coping at this stage. From the viewpoint of the helper, there is a particular need, on the one hand, to facilitate the release and exploration of thoughts and feelings (especially feelings), whilst on the other hand avoiding dependency. Indeed, the value of a helping contract becomes especially clear when dependency problems begin to arise.

Several sets of techniques have been developed to help a person explore his thoughts and feelings in such a way as to increase his mastery of them. Some of these will be described in detail later in this book (see especially pages 143–155).

Our experience suggests that transactional analysis and cognitive re-structuring are especially powerful techniques for developing an under-standing of the thoughts characteristic of this phase and for increasing mastery. Acting-out and fantasy role-play (see discussion of these on page 150) are also useful to achieve these same aims in relation to feelings.

A point worth stressing to those who do find themselves as helpers is that the task is to encourage the release of emotion and of negative thoughts so that the person can experience anger, anxiety, tearfulness, guilt, shame, frustration, pain and worry. It may be necessary to confront the outward coping behaviour of the person so as to permit those expressions, but this will need to be achieved within a relationship of empathy, warmth and acceptance.

Stage 3: Consolidation

The final stage of this adaptation and coping process involves the integration of the new experiences and emotions into a new view of the identity of the person which in turn leads to a new energy for both self and others. The personal anxiety, emotionality and disorientation characteris-tic of the previous stage is greatly reduced and may, in a few, be gone altogether. It is replaced by a new drive and determination to carry on living life to the full.

Not all individuals will reach this stage. Some may be blocked by their failure to work through emotions and thoughts at the previous stage, whilst others will retreat to depression or repression. But when this stage is reached, the worry work and anxiety will prove invaluable as strength-ening experiences.

At this stage it is time for helpers to withdraw and to recognize that the person must not only feel stronger and more independent but must also be independent. No matter how long *or short* the helping process has been, integration leads to the cessation of direct helping.

Coping and the Child of Separation

Earlier we briefly mentioned some specified changes which affect children 'caught' in a divorce or separation. It is necessary to elaborate upon the impact of divorce on children and to identify some specific roles and tasks for helpers.

The first point to make is that, just as the adults are involved in the three-stage coping and adaptation process outlined above, children too are involved in this process. Not only do they often act as catalysts for the coping problems of both their custodial and non-custodial parents, they also experience a similar coping process themselves. That this is sometimes an extremely difficult process for children is hardly surprising for two reasons. First, the coping with separation process occurs during the period of major development for children. Young children are often in the process of discovering their identity when the stability of the identity is challenged by the separation. Adolescents are in the process of discovering their social roles and are moving towards maturity when these developments are interrupted by a breach of social roles which is, in some communities at least, regarded as a symbol of the immaturity of their parents. The combination of coping with normal development and coping with divorce is too much for some and leads to behavioural, attitudinal or emotional change. Second, children are often kept in the dark about what is happening both prior to and after the divorce. Attempts to 'protect' children by keeping them in ignorance of the fundamental shifts in the family and of the causes of these shifts, and by shielding them from emotions, often lead them towards the assumption that they are the cause. Ignorance breeds suspicion and suspicion breeds blame.

Stuart Fine, a Canadian psychiatrist, has explored the impact of divorce on children. He notes particularly that reactions to divorce and separation amongst children are directly related to age. We give below a brief summary of his findings:

Children aged 2½–8: These children feel strongly that, somehow, they have been the cause of the separation and this leads them to a pervasive sadness about themselves and their effect on their parents and towards their custodial and non-custodial parent.

Children 9–12: Whilst they may be more aware of the reasons for their parents' separation, they feel a shame about the fact that it has happened at all. This feeling of being ashamed acts to inhibit them from sharing their thoughts and feelings with their own friends and confidants. In short, the shame promotes repression. This repression often shows itself in behavioural changes – such as increased truancy or more headaches, stomach aches or reported back pains or underachievement at school.

Adolescents: Older children begin to be concerned with their own prospects in relation to marriage. In particular, they seek to identify the problems that lead to the separation of their parents and to examine the extent to which their own handling of that problem would have led to a similar problem. To be sure, they use their parents as a model of marriage and explore the "goodness of a fit" between themselves and that model. In addition, adolescents are generally in the process of exploring their own sexuality. If their custodial parent is in the process of rediscovering his or her own sexuality and is seeking re-marriage, then the adolescents' sexual values may prove a source of concern for both them and their parents.

Clearly, these descriptions are of responses to separation which can be viewed either as being or having the potential of being maladaptive. We have already documented some positive feelings that children can and do experience (see pages 56–57). It should also be clear that the age clarification used here is tentative – meant to indicate a stage in the child's development rather than a precise chronological age.

The implications of research findings such as those reported by Fine and others, especially Michael Rutter, is that the children of a divorcing family need to be involved in both pre-divorce and post-divorce helping. They need to be present in discussions about their future and involved in the adaptation and coping process that follows separation itself. They need to be enabled to express their anger, hurt and other feelings. Such involvement is intended to enable them both to develop their own coping repertoire whilst at the same time becoming more aware both of the reasons for the separation and of the problems this gives rise to for others. Whilst their involvement may initially inhibit the adaptation and coping process, it is essential if they are not to experience undue disturbance in their own thoughts, feelings and actions.

Conclusions

Divorce and separation are facts of life. They are more likely to occur to a given family than a road accident. In this chapter we have sought to document why divorce occurs, how it occurs and what the consequences of divorce can be. No two people will experience divorce in exactly the same way and not all these experiences have been or can be documented here. It should be clear, however, that divorce carries many crisis possibilities, and that, with thoughtful help warmly given, it can also be regarded as a vehicle for positive change.

CHAPTER 5

BEING YOUNG IN AN OLD COMMUNITY – ADOLESCENCE AND CRISIS

Introduction

Whilst many other chapters in this book concentrate upon crisis events, this chapter examines some of the developmental crises that may occur during adolescence. We emphasize that these '*may*' occur, since there is little evidence that crises due to development are an inevitability during pre- and early adulthood. What is more, the experience of adolescence for many is not crisis-laden, but better described as a series of transitional events which are managed with varying degrees of coping competence. Indeed, some young people only discover that their adolescence was potentially crisis-laden when they read about this period of development in sociological or psychological accounts of adolescent development.

Though the period between eleven and twenty may not lead to crisis, it does carry the potential for crisis. It is for this reason that we include this short chapter in this book. Adolescence also features in a later chapter on unemployment and job-loss. In that chapter it is suggested that 'becoming employed' is an important sign of the young person forging his or her own identity and of the family securing a stable future for its young. This major 'separation-individuation' phase can be thwarted by prolonged youth unemployment. The link between this chapter and that dealing with unemployment is thus an important one. For in that chapter it is implied that social conditions can significantly determine not only whether a person is 'in crisis' or not, but may also determine his development. Psychological development is not just a feature of the person's own psychology, but is strongly related to prevailing social conditions and the degree of social support a person receives.

Ten Crisis Points in Adolescence

In general, young people are resilient. They are able to withstand and cope with many changes and uncertainties. They need to cope both with changes in social expectations of them and with changes in their physical and emotional make-up, and many are well equipped psychologically and phsycially for these changes. But there are studies which show that some adolescents are less able to cope with change and uncertainty than others and that most adolescents experience difficulties with some aspect of their development. Though most experience 'difficulties', it is not clear how many experience crisis.

Reviewing the available research (see Boorer and Murgatroyd, 1973) on the difficulties faced by adolescents leads to the suggestion that there are ten potential 'stressors' not essentially connected with biological development which give rise to concern. These are:

1 A feeling that they are falling short of expectations and standards.

2 An uncertainty and sometimes a fear of future choices.

3 A feeling of being fragmented – feeling that they are not a whole person, but not knowing how to become whole.

4 Feeling too dependent upon the decisions, thoughts, feelings and actions of others (especially adults), coupled with a feeling of being unable to break out of this dependence.

5 Being unwilling to set limits or rule things out, even though the need for limits is clearly recognized.

6 Being unsure about job-futures even when in work.

7 Being unsure about sex-roles and sexual behaviour.

8 Finding it difficult to make and sustain significant (non-trivial) relationships with others.

9 Finding it difficult to cope with the range of emotions which seem to arise out of consciousness.

10 Finding it difficult to accept responsibility.

As is clear, many of these potential stressors concern the young person's relationship to the community and his elders (especially points 1, 2, 4 and 6), whilst others relate to his own self-concept and development. This distinction between self-concerns and community concerns will be used throughout this chapter, though it should be recognized that these concerns are inextricably related.

Community Concerns

In an unpublished study, Stephen Murgatroyd asked young people to document in their own words their perceptions of the way in which older persons saw them. Three clear views emerged. The first view, held by the majority of the 200 young people (aged fourteen – nineteen) of both sexes who participated in the study, might best be described as the 'victim' view. According to this view, young people are caught in the middle of a 'catch 22' or 'vicious circle' situation. They are not adults, but are expected to behave like adults; when they behave like the adults in their own lives (parents, teachers, employers) they are told that they are not adults and should act according to their age. These young people typically report confusion about their roles in the family, in the community and in institutions (especially schools). In particular, they feel that they are being encouraged to be assertive and discouraged from achieving assertiveness. In the study, 58% of the 200 young people shared this 'victim' perspective.

A second group identified in this study is best characteried as *'perse-cuted'*. Here, the perception of themselves as 'victim' goes further than that of the previous group. For this group regard themselves not only as being caught in a 'catch-22' situation, but also they feel themselves to be persecuted by adults for being young. One young person said:

> Look, there are some people I have to talk to, right, who just don't like young people. They think we're scum, right. So the game is beat these people at their own game. When they're being nasty to me I am nasty to them. When they are nice to me, I am nasty to them – 'cos whatever they are, that's how I see them.

This view, held by 5% of the young people studied, is most common amongst those young people who have committed delinquent acts or who are regarded by their peers as excessively negativistic. They are 'against' older people in principle because they see older people to be against them. This group do not account for all the delinquents who were a part of this study. Some who had convictions for vandalism, assault or theft explained their behaviour in terms of 'having fun' and in terms of seeking excitement. This group of 'fun through deviance' young people came from all three groups identified in this study and rarely articulated clear reasons for their delinquent acts, perhaps because the acts as such had no 'reason'.

The remaining 37% of those studied by Murgatroyd are described as 'enthusiasts'. They are not that concerned with the image of society that they have or with the image that society has of them. They are most concerned with their own lives, their own circle of friends and their own careers, either as students or young workers (or both). They are so enthusiastic about what they are doing and what they are about to do that it seems as if they are oblivious of the community and its effects upon them. Whilst they recognize the contributions individual adults make to their well-being, they do not regard them as other than contributors – they are not the basis for a view of the community which they hold or are formulating.

This study does not suggest that these three groups have different strategies for coping with the effects of the community upon them – no substantial data was collected from these young people concerning their coping behaviours. But it is clear from these descriptions that two of these groups ('persecuted' and 'enthusiasts') do adopt different strategies for coping with the community in which they live. The enthusiasts ignore the community unless it is valuable to their purposes. The persecuted attack the community since they see the community to be attacking them.

Whilst this study is a relatively small one, it does suggest two points for those who are seeking to help young people to cope with their feelings about the community. First, they need to understand the way in which the young person views the community. This study identifies three major community views – but there may be many more. It is clear from the descriptions provided here that reactions to the community are as much a function of the way the young person views the community as the actual behaviours members of the community engage in towards that young person. Helpers need to understand that young person's views before they can understand that person's needs, interests, difficulties and crises.

A second point for helpers concerns the ways in which the perceptions of the community which the young person has can be changed. Adult helpers often seek to encourage young people to develop a view of the community which is essentially their own. They fail to recognize both that their own view of the place of the individual in the community is not shared by many young people and that the view of an adult necessarily differs from the views of young people who are seeking to become adult. The helper's task is to understand the young person's views 'as if' they were the helper's own without losing the 'as if' quality (empathy) whilst at the same time encouraging the young person to test the reality of his perceptions against his own experience. Facilitating change is not synonymous with the task of 'conversion'. For the changes which helpers most often seek are best achieved through enabling the young person to see, examine, experience and adopt other views of the community.

About Careers

A significant difficulty faced by many young people concerns the transition from school to work or non-work. Though certain aspects of this important event will be examined in the later chapter on unemployment, some points are necessary here.

Beginning work is a challenge. For not only do young people constantly assess their work against their view of what work should be, they are also tested time and again by the adults at work. The trainee nurse who is asked to 'go down to the stores to fetch a Fallopian tube' or the garage hand who is asked to fetch an 'air hook' or the apprentice carpenter who is asked to fetch a glass hammer – all are being tested for tolerance and being reminded of their place at work as 'novice'. At work they are still cast as learner – a role they were used to as school students and which they saw entry to work as ending. Being a 'learner-worker' is sometimes stressful, not only because learning generally carries the potential of stress but also because the young worker seems to feel strongly the fear of failure.

Fear of failure is an established stressor for young people. It concerns not only the fear of failure in the performance of some task but also the fear of failing to meet the expectations of others. It is a motive evident in worker-learners as well as school and college students. But it goes further for some. Fear of failure also encompasses the fear of failing to meet their own expectations for themselves. This is a particularly strong motive for young people (see McClelland, 1965) and can be a source of much stress and conflict. Many jobs are not experienced in the same way that young people anticipate and many more are simply the only jobs available to the young person, no matter what their ambitions or expectations. The fear of failure is a stressor that can give rise to conflict and crisis.

Many jobs involve choices. Choices about training, about which particular organization to give service to and which particular person or group within that organization to owe loyalty to – all are examples of choices at work. All jobs have other choices: to work hard or not, to leave or stay, to change jobs or move locations but keep the same job. These choices are also potentially stressful, especially given the feeling that the 'wrong' choice can have dire consequences. In part these worries about making wrong choices occur because of the lack of choice young people have whilst engaged in compulsory schooling and whilst in the control of their parents. Choice rarely characterizes the world of the school student; most of the choices students can make are not substantive and have marginal consequences. The responsibility for making choices is given suddenly to young people. Helpers can therefore facilitate choice through enabling the young person to develop decision-making skills and to recognize their assertive rights (see Chapter 11).

Another concern about work which many young people have relates to their uncertainty about sex roles. Many work environments bring young people into closer and more open contact with members of the opposite sex and these contacts give rise to sex-related issues. Equally important, the work environment can (depending upon circumstances) make possible contact with a variety of males and females across a wide age-range and this can lead to questions about the nature of appropriate behaviour towards colleagues of either sex. Some young people find the informality of many work environments difficult; others enjoy this informality, though still find it necessary to adjust their understanding of the nature of interpersonal relationships at work. The point here is that the relationships young people enter into at work are different from those entered into in the family or at school. Adjustment is necessary. Not all can make these adjustments easily.

But perhaps the most important stressor relates to work itself. Many people are, according to Paul Willis (1979), 'born to labour' – they have little choice over the occupations they enter which are determined by the occupations of their parents, their geographic locations and their schooling. Ken Roberts, a sociologist working in Liverpool, has shown clearly that the freedom of choice of occupation is severely limited for the majority of young people and that the idea that job-chances are related to individual abilities is both mythical and damaging. Yet young people are encouraged, in education and through advertising, to believe that occupational choice is possible – even at a time when unemployment is high. This conflict between social expectations – heavily supported through institutions within the community – and reality is often stressful. Educational guidance workers and educational counsellors spend some considerable time helping individual students and potential students to cope with the discovery that their expectations cannot be realized. Whilst some, like Professor Peter Daws working in Northern Ireland, dispute this argument and suggest that young people are enabled by their education to make real and meaningful career choices, the evidence produced by Roberts and his followers seems convincing. Many young people are frustrated by the social structure from entering occupations which they desire and are often qualified for and this frustration can be stressful for some.

These observations about possible stressors at work, like those made about the stressors young people see in the community, suggest potential crisis points for young people which arise from their social position. As was made clear at the beginning of this chapter, many young people cope adequately with these stressors. But those who fail to cope often experience these stressors in terms of crisis.

Self-concerns

Many of the concerns about community outlined briefly above come back to three central questions which young people are seen to ask. These are:

1 What is my status now and how does this relate to the status I thought I would have at this time?
2 Am I now able to act more independently as an adult would or am I still constrained in the way I feel I have been in the past?
3 What is my role in relation to others?

Whilst these questions are not unique to young people, they do provide an agenda for examining the community concerns which many young people express.

Behind this agenda is a concern with 'self' – with both the way in which the young person feels in control of his 'self' and the way in which this self meets his own expectations and desires. Also, the young person is exploring thoughts and feelings about self in many areas – relationships to authority, friendships, sexuality, towards political or social questions, about learning, and about the future. In short, the period of adolescence is seen by many psychologists as characterized by a concern with self-esteem and self-understanding. It is a reflective period and a period in which the young person often experiments with images of himself as expressed emotionally through relationships and actions and physically through sexual behaviour and dress.

Sometimes the concern with self-understanding becomes obsessive. Young people become concerned that the gap between their 'ideal' self and their 'actual' self is so great that they feel they do not like themselves – their self-worth is low. For others, the concern with self leads to an ending of relationships with long-established friends and to changes in the nature of relationships within the family. These losses sometimes are felt as painful and may lead to a lowering of self-esteem. For those who find the agenda for becoming independent arduous and the task of achieving separation from dependencies painful, there may be many sudden and unexpected changes of mood. These difficulties can and do lead young people to reject offers of help from both adults and their peers. They feel that 'others' (and this can include almost anyone) lack rapport with their own thoughts and feelings and they seek to resolve their inner conflicts and pain on their own.

Indeed, this desire to minimize the amount of external help in resolving inner conflicts is a part of the problem of adolescence. A study of young people in the United States and Denmark conducted by the Harvard Laboratory of Human Development showed that less than 40% of those questioned would seek advice and help from others. A recent study of young people in Scotland (Siann, Draper and Cosford, 1982) suggests that the figure in Britain may be higher, especially for parents. But the fact remains that adults do not figure prominently in the helping resources chosen and used by young people. When the reasons for this are explored, three key points are mentioned by young people. These are: (a) that they do not feel that many adults understand their problems from their point of view – they are seen to show little empathy; (b) that they advise young people to do things which they would not do themselves – there is a lack of congruence between the advice and behaviour of adults; and (c) that many adults treat the problems young people have as being either trivial or as being unworthy of any real in-depth discussion – there is a lack of warmth and genuineness. These three points of complaint – cited in many studies (see Roberts, et al. 1982) – suggest that helpers are viewed pragmatically by young people. Helpers need to accept them as persons and help given needs to be genuinely and warmly offered and be empathetic. These are necessary, and in some cases sufficient, conditions for helping a young person come to terms with self-doubts, feelings of poor self-esteem and lack of self-worth.

Conclusion

This chapter has examined, albeit briefly, some of the common concerns of young people in terms of both community and self. In addition, the need for genuineness, warmth and empathy in those who wish to help young people cope with a period which can be stressful and crisis-laden has been emphasized.

Adolescence is not a crisis for most young people, but can become crisis-laden if their concerns with community and/or self are obsessive and they feel isolated and unable to receive the help they occasionally desire. It is important to recognize that normal development can involve crisis – a point stressed in Chapter 3. Those who seek to help those in crisis can do much to help young people avoid crisis during adolescence.

CHAPTER 6

GROWING OLD OR OLDER AND GROWING – CRISIS AND OLD AGE

Introduction

Being old is not a crisis. Indeed, many people in their sixties, seventies and eighties regard this period of their life as rich in terms of experience and full in terms of relationships. Many have grandchildren whom they are able to enjoy without feeling the responsibilities of parenthood. Others develop new friendships or pursue hobbies more vigorously. Yet others use the opportunities afforded by retirement to begin new pastimes and explore new forms of part-time work. Retirement and pensionhood can be exciting and invigorating.

But some experience retirement and ageing as stressful and crisis-laden. They feel that the changes in their physical selves represent a deterioration and they find this stressful. They feel that they have fewer people able to support them. They feel that the friendships, certainties and rewards of work are gone and will not be replaced in retirement – this they find stressful. Some find the change from work to non-work in retirement has the consequences of severely reducing their weekly income, and this they find stressful. Others notice that more and more of their friends and relatives die or become ill and the anticipation of their own death or of the possibility of illness is felt as stressful. Others have to be rehoused at the death of their husband or wife or are placed in nursing homes following illness – this too can be stressful. Whilst ageing and retirement are not necessarily stressful experiences, this period of life (as with many others) carries the potential for crisis and this is why this chapter is included in this book.

The aim of this chapter is to document the sources of crisis for older people. In particular, the chapter will examine crises which arise from physical changes in the person, from changes in their relationships with the community, from changes in their thinking processes and from changes in their emotional and personal states. Some particular tasks for helpers are identified, together with some of the difficulties which helpers typically experience in their attempts to help older people. This chapter has been particularly influenced by work within the Open University on courses dealing with retirement and ageing and by several studies which suggest that ageing does not lead to deteriorating intellectual abilities.

Physical Changes

Bodily changes do occur with age, and we shall list some of them below. Before doing so, it is important to note that there is no fixed age at which some of these changes will occur and no certainty that they will occur at all. Each person is physically unique and his or her body will respond differently both to the process of ageing and the consequences of illness or accidents. Thus, it is important to recognize that there are individual differences in the way in which people experience the process of ageing. These individual differences make it possible for some to look and feel old at forty and for others to undergo hardly any physical or emotional changes from the age of forty onwards. The changes we list below are therefore an indication of a range of possible physical changes which relate to ageing. In reading this list, it is important for helpers to note that it is often more important to consider the way people feel and think about these changes occuring in them than it is to examine the actual changes themselves.

The list we provide here comes from a variety of sources, including psychological and medical accounts of ageing. The list covers changes in appearance, in the bones, in the ability of the older person to adjust to temperature, in digestion, in the brian and in the senses.

1 *Changes in appearance* – An obvious change for many people concerns the skin and general appearance. Hair greys, the skin wrinkles and facial flabbiness occurs. The body seems to 'loose its bloom', with the skin sometimes becoming paler and blotchier in places. Skin changes are largely due to changes in the levels of fatty substances in the skin which in turn affect the skin's ability to hold water. As a person gets older, the skin loses some of its elasticity. Some older people like some of these changes – they feel more 'distinguished looking' – whilst

others regard them as a sign of deterioration and see themselves as becoming increasingly unlike their former selves.

2 *Changes in bone-brittleness* – For many people, losing the last of their own teeth is regarded as a sign of ageing. In most cases, however, it is more of a sign of a sugar-full diet and poor dental care. But it is the case that teeth will be more problematic for the older person. This is the case for the bones generally – the bones become a little more brittle, thus increasing the chance of breakage. Bone-joints become stiffer, leading to an increase in the incidence of arthritic complaints and a reduction in the person's freedom of movement. According to a study by P.H.N. Wood, undertaken for the British League Against Rheumatism, 41% of persons aged sixty-five or over have some form of arthritic complaint compared to 23% of those aged between forty-five and sixty-four. Severe arthritis can be disabling, leading the person to have difficulty with bathing, preparing meals, shopping, climbing stairs, getting in and out of bed, doing housework, getting out of the house and with using buses. No drugs can give complete relief and some of the drugs which have been used do have side-effects which are a cause of some concern. These observations make it clear that substantial changes in a person's physical condition can be stressful.

3 *Changes in responsiveness to temperature* – As a person gets older, their ability to regulate their body temperature declines a little. This leads older people to feel changes in temperature more acutely than their younger counterparts and leads to an especial difficulty in coping with cold. A considerable number of older people die each year of hypothermia – a condition caused solely by temperature changes.

4 *Changes in digestion* – There is relatively little evidence that a person's digestive system changes with ageing. This may seem surprising, since changes in the digestive system seem to be a major conversation topic with many old people. What does seem to be the case is that the digestive system is most sensitive to changes in emotional state – to mood, stress, anger, sadness, frustration. Some have suggested that older people are more sensitive to their emotional state and that this sensitivity may then affect their digestive systems.

5 *Changes in the senses* – Many people harbour fears about the impact of ageing upon their sight, hearing and other senses. There is little convincing evidence of systematic and predictable changes in the senses which result solely from getting older. Though it is possible for some to

experience sense-deterioration (especially in hearing and sight), this deterioration is likely to be slight. A wise seventy-five-year-old pointed out, though, that 'it is sometimes useful to use age as a reason for not hearing things like "will you do the washing up, grandad?" and to pretend to strain hard to hear things you want to hear, like who won the Grand National!' This is not to say that older people do not experience difficulties with sight or hearing or smell or touch. They do. But it is not possible to attribute most of these difficulties simply to the fact of getting older.

6 *Changes in the brain* – There is no evidence that ageing inevitably leads to a reduction in the ability of the brain to function. The memory, perception, conceptual skills and thinking processes can remain sharp through to death at ninety or older. There is, however, evidence that these functions of the brain decline with lack of practice. An older person who remains intellectually active will retain his general intellectual abilities. A person who regularly uses his memory will retain the ability to do so. A person who regards age as a reason for not engaging in intellectual, creative or memory-related tasks will find that these activities become harder to engage in.

7 *Changes in the circulatory system* – The circulatory system is the rather clumsy name for the blood-supply system of the body. Almost all of us will be affected by hardening of the arteries in old age (the medical terms for this is arteriosclerosis or atherosclerosis). Such hardening of the arteries leads to a thickening of the artery walls and to a consequent reduction in the speed at which blood circulates around the body. This can lead to blood-clots being formed and to these clots either blocking an artery or causing an obstruction elsewhere in the body (e.g., heart, lung, brain and lower limbs). It is important to recognize that the changes in the circulatory system can lead to tiredness, lack of energy and occassional difficulties in breathing. Whilst these changes can be coped with by reductions in the level of bodily activity engaged in, the older person who experiences circulatory problems often develops a fear of consequences and this fear can be stressful.

These seven areas of change can all have consequences for the person which can be stressful. Often more important, though, are the old person's experiences of physical illness. Arthritis has already been mentioned (see point 2 above), and this illness can be seriously debilitating. Two other illnesses are common amongst older people. These are: (a) a stroke and its consequences, and (b) incontinence. We discuss both briefly below.

The Royal College of Physicians has defined a stroke as 'an acute disturbance of cerebral (brain) function . . . lasting more than 24 hours'. The following table from the Royal College of Physicians (1974) shows the relationship between age and the incidence of strokes.

Table 6.1   The Incidence of Stroke Illness Related to Age

Age Group	Annual incidence per 1000 population
35–44	0.25
45–54	1.00
55–64	3.500
65–74	9.00
75–84	20.00
85+	40.00

As is clear from this table, a great many older people are likely to suffer from a stroke and its consequences. One set of consequences of a stroke is often a paralysis of a limb or set of limbs, disordered thoughts and confused speech. Some other consequences are:

1 Loss of the sense of touch (medically called stereognosis).

2 Loss of a sensation of position in relation to space – which makes movement and balance difficult.

3 Loss of all forms of sensation in areas under paralysis.

4 Loss of different sensations in different areas of the body. For example touch and movement could be lost down one side of the body whilst feelings of pain or sensitivity to temperature could be lost down the other.

A stroke is a serious illness, which gives rise to stress in both the affected person and those close to that person.

The second illness which particularly affects older persons is incontinence. According to a study by Brockelhurst, who interviewed 557 elderly persons living at home, 17% of men and 23% of women claimed a degree of urinary incontinence. Though the degree of incontinence differed from person to person, it is clearly a serious problem for older persons. What is more, it is not a problem that they find it easy to talk about or to admit, even to doctors. There is a sense of shame associated with the illness – the person feels as if he should be in control of his bladder – and a general lack of recognition of the status of incontinence as an illness in its own right. Incontinence, in our experience, is a particularly distressing phenomenon, both for the persons affected and those with whom they share their lives.

Just as illnesses are important to a person's physical condition, so too are accidents. Just taking one set of accidents – those involving a fall of some kind – the incidence is quite staggering. According to a study by Gryfe and his co-workers (Gryfe, 1977), 70% of retired persons are likely to experience a fall which leads to some consequential injury. Gryfe's study was conducted in a residential home especially designed to minimize the risk of falls. The researchers comment that the incidence of falls in an open community must be at least the same, 'if not greater'. A fall can be both physically damaging and psychologically disturbing – it is seen by many as a further sign that they are loosing control of their bodies. For there is now evidence that many falls are due to a physiological decline simply connected with ageing. Older people feel the change in their ability to control their bodies and the limits their bodies impose upon their functioning both as an enforced change in their behaviours and a sign of deteriorating independence and identity. Falls, illnesses and physical changes can be stressful and painful.

Older people make use of proprietry drugs to help alleviate the pain of illness. Often, they are reluctant to see doctors or to take drugs prescribed by doctors, preferring drugs they can buy over the counter which have attractive advertised qualities. In addition, there is evidence that older people tend to obtain more drugs than their symptoms actually require – they often take drugs prescribed by doctors in addition to those available over the counter from chemists. The result can be that some older people are taking between three and nine different types of drugs. Also, there is some evidence that older people are not always fully aware either of the correct dosage for some of the drugs they take or of the specific purposes for which they are taking them. Helpers can provide valuable assistance to older people by checking the dosage of drugs they offer, by clarifying their purposes and by ensuring that the drugs are not being taken in combinations with other drugs which either counteract their effects or interact to produce unwanted reactions.

This section of this chapter has documented some of the physical changes which take place through ageing and has briefly documented some of the illnesses to which older people are particularly prone. But it would not be right to give the impression of inevitable decay, illness and deterioration. The following was written by Carl Rogers, one of the world's leading psychotherapists, who is still working at seventy-nine. In describing the physical effects of ageing upon himself, he says this:

> I do feel physical deterioration. I notice it in many ways. Ten years ago I greatly
> enjoyed throwing a frisbee (a plastic discus). Now my right shoulder is so painfully arthritic that this kind of activity is out of the question. In my garden I realize that a task which would have been easy five years ago, but difficult last year, now seems like too much, and I had better leave it for my once-a-week gardener. This slow deterioriation, with various minor disorders of vision, heartbeat and the like, informs me that the physical portion of what I call 'me' is not going to last for ever.
> Yet I still enjoy a four-mile walk along the beach. I can lift heavy objects, do all the shopping, cooking and dishwashing when my wife is ill, carry my own luggage without puffing. The female form still seems to me one of the loveliest creations of the universe, and I appreciate it greatly. I feel as sexual in my interests as I was at thirty-five, though I can't say the same about my ability to perform. . . . So I am well aware that I am obviously old. Yet from the inside I'm still the same person in many ways, neither old nor young.

(Carl Rogers, 1980, *A Way of Being*, Boston: Houghton-Mifflin Co, pp. 71–72.)

This extract suggests that the feelings about the physical effects of ageing are an important feature of the feeling of being old. Whilst physical deterioration will occur for many, it is the way that physical change is interpreted and understood that significantly affects the person. The task of the helper is to help older persons understand more fully what is happening to them and to encourage them to share their thoughts and feelings about the changes their bodies are undergoing.

Changed Community Relationships

There are many assumptions about ageing that have a wide currency in the community. Two such assumptions are that: (a) intellectual abilities (i.e., capacity for learning and memory) decline with age and (b) that older people are less creative and imaginative than younger or middle-aged persons. There are many other assumptions of this kind, but these two illustrate the point. These assumptions become the taken-for-granted assumptions on which many actions are based. Many organizations which aim to provide educational services, for example, do not advertise directly to pensioner groups. Many social organizations find retired persons know little about them, suggesting that their services are directly aimed at groups other than older persons. Many individuals act towards older people as if such assumptions about illness outlined here were true. Yet there is little evidence to support these assumptions. Memory does not decline with age but does decline with lack of practice; ability to learn follows a similar rule. Many older people also act as if these assumptions were true – the phrase 'you can't teach an old dog new tricks' symbolizes the fact that such views are enshrined in the folklore of ageing.

The point being made here is that the actions of older people are not independent of the views held by the community concerning the nature and implications of ageing. In looking at crises that affect old people it is necessary to take into account the extent to which community assumptions about the effects of ageing are a part of the 'problem' that the person is experiencing. The way in which a person's actions are being shaped by the community in which he is placed can mean the difference between growing old or getting older and continuing to grow intellectually.

One particular social attitude that seems to affect the older person powerfully is the attitude towards the older person working. Many feel that the fact of retirement indicates that the person has reached the end of his useful working life. Yet many older people have been retired from work not because they were no longer able to perform their duties or because they were using methods of work that were outdated, but because the agreement that their company had reached with their unions required retirement at a particular age. Many High Court judges in the United Kingdom, Supreme Court judges in the USA, Presidents of the USA and leaders of political parties throughout the world are over the normal age of retirement. Carl Rogers, mentioned earlier in this chapter, continues to work at the age of seventy-nine and is no less persuasive because he is old. Many clergy work and are effective until late old age and monarchs generally go on being monarchs until death. Yet carpenters, plumbers, engineers and many other 'blue-collar' workers are retired at sixty or sixty-five and find getting casual work difficult, despite the fact that they remain skilled and able to work. This rejection of their abilities to labour is a source of stress for some – especially those for whom work has provided a major rationale for their life.

Just as social attitudes can affect older people and shape their behaviour and thoughts, so too can social conditions. Many older people find that the reduction of their income from a wage to an allowance affects their standards of living. This is particularly true of those workers who do not belong to pension schemes or to superannuation schemes which provide both cash sums on retirement and a regular allowance. Those whose sole income derives from the State face a relative decline of income in retirement. State pensions are rarely adequate to meet normal living expenses for those who do not own their own homes and for those who have substantial fuel bills. Inflation is a socio-economic phenomenon which particularly affects the old on a fixed income. For some, retirement means relative poverty. They seek to save on heating bills by not using their heating systems, thus increasing the risk of hypothermia. They seek to economize on household expenses by reducing the level of their food purchases, thus reducing their bodies' ability to withstand illness. They seek to minimize their outgoings by reducing their level of social contact with others and by staying at home rather than travelling out, thus increasing feelings of isolation. In short, the financial position of older people – essentially a social policy decision – affects their thoughts, feelings and actions. Furthermore, a social policy to maintain the level of State support for persons in retirement at rates lower than (say) the minimum wage can be a source of considerable distress.

Other social conditions affect the way an elderly person thinks, feels and acts. For example, some older people are not as able to look after and decorate their dwellings in the ways that they have been used to and yet are not able to afford to pay for the costs of decorations or repairs by others. Some older people, on the death of their spouses, find themselves forced to be rehoused or placed in residential care. These features of living can be distressing, especially since the move from one's own home into residential care is viewed by many as a loss of independence and the beginning of increasing dependency, the outcome of which is inevitably death.

Finally, the social attitudes and social conditions which affect older persons also affect the older person's family and their ability to care for their parents or near relatives. Social attitudes and conditions encourage geographic mobility, smaller family size, a greater dependence upon state aid for medical, convalescent and care conditions, as well as financial independence of family groupings within a family network. All of these features of the social conditions of the families of older persons can affect the degree of social support that the older person receives from those from whom they may have expected such support. Whilst the degree to which these social conditions affect families will vary from area to area and from culture to culture, there is some evidence that older persons experience less social support from their families now than was the case some two decades ago. The feeling that they are not in a position to call upon family, but yet want to do so, can be distressing for many older persons. The needs of elderly persons and the demands they can make upon families are also sources of crises for many family members.

Thoughts and Feelings

In describing the physical changes that may occur in old age, it was noted that the way in which a person thinks and feels about these changes is often as important as the changes themselves. Greying hair can be regarded as the 'final straw', indicating that ageing is now beginning to 'take its toll', or it can be regarded as a signal of some new, more distinctive and distinguished appearance. Thinking about physical changes can often determine how these changes are experienced.

Just as this point about the perception of change is important for understanding the way in which a person reacts to physical change, so too is it important in understanding the ways in which an older person comes to terms with learning, thinking and feeling. For older persons wishing to learn a skill or to develop an understanding of some subject have to overcome not only the problems inherent in a particular piece of learning but also the social attitudes which imply that learning in old age becomes increasingly difficult. The way they think about learning can affect the way in which they learn. If they believe that learning will be difficult because they are old, then this may be a source of crisis for them, since frustration is a frequent beginning point for crises.

Two common assumptions about the intellect are associated with ageing. The first is that as a person gets older his memory declines. The second assumption is that concentration is more difficult for older persons than for younger persons. Neither of these assumptions are true in this way. As has already been mentioned, memory does not decline with age but seems to decline with lack of practice. There are also a number of different kinds of memory – short-term memory, long-term memory and immediate memory – and a decline in one due to lack of practice does not automatically lead to a decline in the others. Also, what matters most in many situations requiring memory is motivation – if the need is strong enough, most people will have effective memories. What is true is that many people have exaggerated views of how good their memories used to be. In relation to concentration, there is a considerable degree of confusion about what concentration actually is (Apter and Murgatroyd, 1980) and dispute about how it might be measured (Apter and Murgatroyd, 1976). But the evidence seems to suggest that many persons of all ages have difficulty in concentration – this being a difficulty often cited by students (Murgatroyd, 1982), no matter how old they might be.

But more important than whether the memory or concentration or other intellectual processes do in fact decline with age is the fear that they might. Many elderly persons fear embarking upon some tasks (i.e., following a course of study, reading a very long novel, becoming involved in drama, political activity) simply because they do not think that they will be able to retain their memory or concentration to the level required. They fear failure and do not engage in action. The fear of possible failure inhibits the way in which they engage with others. This fear of failure can also be a source for distress.

In terms of emotions, there is some limited evidence that older persons feel their emotions more intensely than younger people and they are more likely to be emotionally labile. This means that older people are more likely to feel themselves switching between one emotion and another and feel these switches more strongly than they used to. It is as if there is an added degree of sensitivity to even slight changes in emotional condition. It was noted earlier that emotional states (anger, depression, sadness) affect physical actions such as the digestive system. Increased emotional lability can lead to an increase in the experience of emotional and physical distress.

Two particular emotional phenomena are noticeable in older people. The first is depression. Older people are more likely to move in a circle in which illness and death occur than, say, people of age twenty–thirty years. This can be distressing and lead the person to experience fears about both his ill or dying friends and about his own former health and vitality. Older people report a higher incidence of depression than younger people and receive a higher proportion of prescriptions for drugs to alleviate depression, sleeplessness and anxiety than any other age group (Bergman, 1971). The second emotional phenomena frequently reported by helpers who work with the older person is a high degree of morbidity – a preoccupation with death. Though such a preoccupation is not surprising – death is imminent for some older persons – it can lead to emotional distress, undereating and disturbed sleep. The unwillingness of many friends and relatives to share their thoughts and feelings about death (see Chapter 9) often contributes to rather than alleviates the distress to which morbidity can give rise.

Helping Tasks

A large number of voluntary and professional persons have a high degree of committtment to older people. They often report some difficulties in helping. One of the commonest concerns deafness – many older people do not admit their deafness. This makes conversation and effective communication difficult. Also, many older persons seem to 'ramble' in their speech, being easily side-tracked from the line of their arguments. Whilst this is time consuming and sometimes frustrating for helpers pushed for time, it rarely presents a barrier to helping.

Most significant is the reluctance of many older persons to seek help – personal or medical – at a time when the delivery of helping would be most effective. They cope with distress or illness often by waiting to see if the distress declines or the illness cures itself – in some cases this results in the situation worsening rather than improving.

Also, many older people requiring social action to improve their situation refuse to co-operate since they do not 'want a fuss'. This reluctance to act or to become involved poses a special problem for helpers: should they intervene or should they respect the wishes of the older person and follow their 'instructions'? Whilst many choose to intervene because they, as helpers, consider that the person's long-term interests are best served by such intervention, this view is problematic, especially in relation to intervention in cases of terminal illness. Each helper needs to resolve this issue for himself in the light of the circumstances prevailing in each particular case, but it is not an easy decision.

Conclusion

Not all older people will experience retirement and old age as a crisis. Many will experience this period of their lives as a stimulating and challenging time which brings many rewards. For those that do experience crisis, the personal and social conditions need to be clearly understood by those seeking to help them through their crises. This chapter has attempted to provide a beginning for such understanding.

CHAPTER 7

PARENTING AND HANDICAP – ACCEPTANCE OF THE UNACCEPTABLE

You have just got to accept them for what they are and not keep wishing they were something else, not wishing they were normal. Well, you naturally wish they were normal, but it's no good to keep longing for them to do things you know they cannot do. You have just got to accept them for what they can do.

Introduction

The above quotation comes from the mother of a severely mentally and physically handicapped child. It is given in Hewett's much-cited study, *The Family and the Handicapped Child* (Hewett, 1970). This same book also provides the source for the subtitle of this chapter – chosen here because it accurately evokes the task of coping in the situation in which the parents of a child become aware that their child is mentally or physically handicapped. Though much of the material in this chapter concerns mental handicap – a phenomenon of which one of the authors of this book has considerable personal experience as the parent of a handicapped child – the issues and strategies are much the same as for physical handicap. What is perhaps different is the social awareness of the nature of mental handicap and its implications for parents. All parents of handicapped children face the issue posed by Hewett as their first and final dilemma – how do they accept the unacceptable?

Handicap as Crisis

Before examining the ways in which a person seeks to accept the unacceptable and learns to cope with the fact of handicap, it is helpful to examine the differences between the nature of this crisis and the other crises examined and documented in this text. There are two differences between the crisis experience of the parent faced with handicap and the experience of other crisis. First, the situation of the parent faced with handicap has an objective element – the handicapped child. It is possible to examine the severity of handicap against some standard and to be objective about the implications of the handicap for both the child and the child's parents. Second, unless the child has some gradually deteriorating physical condition which results in death, the object of the problem (the child's handicap) persists during the lifetime of the parents.

The persistence of the problem has both physical and psychological consequences. Emotionally, the individual is faced with the double-edged task of accepting the loss of the 'ideal' child whilst at the same time maintaining responsibility and showing care for the actual child. A number of those who have studied the impact of this upon families have noted that the family becomes increasingly isolated, with many aspects of normal family life being relegated by the 'life of restriction' based around 'the daily grind' of looking after the needs of the child (Young husband *et al.* 1970; Bayley, 1973; Hewett, 1973). Physically, a handicapped child demands more in terms of physical energy of a parent than normal children. What is more, as the child grows older the physical demands often become greater rather than less – the opposite of the situation experienced by the parents of normal children. Parents experience difficulties in taking holidays, in finding babysitters, in getting relief from the daily grind, and these difficulties add to the physical burden handicap can give rise to.

In addition to psychological and physical implications, the parent of a handicapped child also experiences financial consequences of the situation. First, many handicapped children require special equipment, special education and extra care. All of these cost money. Even when state aid is available, it rarely covers the total costs to the parents of the aid they have to provide. Further, some parents experience a loss of earnings, in part because they are often unable to work overtime and in part because the needs of their child often inhibit the return to work of the mother.

Children do not remain babies. They grow, change and develop so that parental acceptance and care cannot be regarded as a temporary burden, but is permanent and often increasing in intensity and range. Thus, the task of coping has to be seen as a moving, dynamic process in which the parents constantly change and adjust to the new demands their growing child makes and to the new situations they find themselves in, given their network of friends and relatives. The most appropriate term to use about the crisis the parents experience is that it is 'recurrent' – the crisis will take many forms, but will recur over the course of the parents' lives.

This brief description of the nature of the parents' experience suggests two points for helpers. First, assisting the person in the resolution of their emotional and psychological reactions to the fact of their child's handicap is but a part of the helper's task. The helper needs to assist the parents to locate help which will enable them to rest and recoup their physical strength. Also, the helper needs to ensure that the benefits and resources of the community are directed towards the needs of these parents. In this circumstance (as with many others) coping with emotions is but a part of the coping task; the parents need to be able to secure resources from the community and campaign for them where the resources are not forthcoming. An undue emphasis upon psychological coping blurs and distorts the reality of coping for the parents of the handicapped child. The recognition of this social aspect to coping gives added emphasis to the work of organizations which campaign on behalf of and actively support parents of handicapped children. It does not take much imagination to see that the provision of such facilities as short-term residential care represents a major need for many families if they are to cope with their own physical and psychological reactions to their situation. Yet, in many locations, such provision has still to be made – suggesting that a part of the helper's task is either to act as advocate for the parents or to enable them to act as advocates for themselves.

Parenting as Crisis

There is a view, advanced by Challela (1981), that any birth – normal or abnormal – is a crisis experience. Parents find themselves in a new situation for which they have had no real training or adequate experience. They find themselves with less time to be themselves, babies and small children taking up a considerable amount of time and energy. Even if the term 'crisis' is regarded as an overstatement, the birth of a child usually represents an important transitional event for a family, with its relationships and structure not being the same again. Parental roles are discovered, relationships within the family are re-aligned, attitudes towards the child and the reactions of others to the child need to be developed, and new financial and practical issues have to be faced.

In terms of the crisis model developed by Caplan, which we presented in Chapter 1, becoming a parent harbours the potential for crisis. For he defines crisis as an upset in the steady state, followed by disorganization leading (if the person is able to restore equilibrium) to development, change and a new form of stability (Caplan, 1968). All who have become parents will recognize elements of this which are familiar. Whilst few would attach the label crisis to their experience, it is clearly an apt label for others.

Perhaps the most important point to note here is that the role of being a parent sometimes gives rise to crisis experiences, but these experiences are a part of the role. For example, Thomas Gordon (Gordon, 1975) speaks of a number of feelings which parents express about being parents. These feelings include: resentment, anger, hostility, aggression, retaliation, dominating, bullying, hating to lose, compliance, withdrawing, escaping, fantasizing, enjoying, cherishing, pleasuring, caring, security, and many others. Some of these feelings evoke crisis, others evoke warmth. Some of these feelings evoke uncertainty, which leads to development and change; others have no long-term impact. As one parent said:

> There are times when I just get so depressed with Mark that I feel like just committing suicide . . . at other times he makes me feel on top of the world . . . I suppose that's what being a parent is like.

This suggests that parenthood is not without crises, but is better characterized as a role in which change is a key characteristic.

Becoming the Parent of a Handicapped Child

The birth of a handicapped child has been described as having a shattering impact upon the parents (Corney, 1981). There is no shortage of literature portraying the variety of emotions that accompany the realization of handicap and the work that parents invest in the task of coping.

In essence, the birth of a handicapped child represents the death of the parents' ideal of what their child was to be and a realization that their lives will not be as free as they had imagined. This loss carries with it an emotional reaction requiring grief work. We describe the process of grief work elsewhere in this book (see pages 112 to 115). Here, there is a need to examine the way in which grieving for the loss of the ideal child is affected by the fact of the birth of a handicapped child.

A major component of the parents' initial reaction to the fact of handicap is one of overwhelming loss – a clear feeling of bereavement following the death of their ideal child. Though helpers may seek to comfort the parents by drawing their attention to the fact of their handicapped child's existence, their new child cannot be accepted until the parents have recognized their loss. Parental reactions at this stage may include denial ('he's not really handicapped' or 'the handicap is only slight, he might grow out of it'), disbelief or anger. Most common is a search for a 'better diagnosis' from the doctor about the nature of the handicap or a more positive prognosis concerning its implications.

Adjustment to a loss of this kind – of an ideal – is difficult to achieve. It can be facilitated by an encouragement to the parents to disclose and share their reactions, especially where these reactions involve guilt, anger, sadness and depression. Grief work requires the parents to work at grieving for their lost ideal as well as to develop an acceptance for the child that is born. Working through the anger and guilt that parents express leads, in the classical grief model suggested by Colin Murray Parkes (1972) and John Bowlby (1980), to a phase of burial in which the expression of painful feelings declines and a gradual acceptance of the objective reality of their situation develops. In the case of handicap, this burial is made more difficult by the constant reminder provided by their actual child of what might have been. A number of researchers have drawn attention to the consequences of failing to work through grief. These consequences can include persistent self-reproach, depression, or outward anger which is frequently directed towards others. The fact of being the parent of a handicapped child makes the burial phase most difficult to achieve. The lost baby becomes a lost five-year-old when the handicap inhibits the child's physical or intellectual development; the lost five-year-old becomes a lost companion on walks or outings where these had hitherto been commonplace. Each point at which the parent recognizes 'what might have been' is a reminder of the loss of the ideal. This has led some writers, notably Olshansky (1962), to use the term 'chronic sorrow' to describe the plight of the parents of a mentally handicapped child. The same term seems appropriate to many parents of physically handicapped children. It implies 'a pervading feeling of psychological grief' – a feeling which is life-long and seems impossible to bury. McCormack, herself the mother of a severely handicapped son, notes that 'you never get over it' (McCormack, 1978) – a view echoed by many parents of children with physical and mental handicaps. The completion of the grief work process is not an easy task.

Helping the Parents Cope

The last section makes clear that the task of emotional adjustment to the fact of handicap is a long-term issue for parents. In this section we wish to examine ways in which they may be helped in this task and some of the issues which parents raise about the help they receive.

At one extreme, Heifitz (1977) has suggested that the emphasis given by helpers to the feelings of the parents is often an indication of the inability of the helper – doctor, social worker, friend, counsellor, health visitor, whoever it might be – to cope with the practical problem the handicap presents. Heifitz suggests that these practical questions – such as ensuring that the parents are given adequate information at each stage of their child's development about the effects of the handicap and that they understand this information – should have priority over the emotional and painful process of grieving, adjustment and coping. Whilst this may seem too harsh a rejection of the work of many helpers, Heifitz's comments do direct attention to the poor quality of the practical service many parents feel they receive.

Parents need three kinds of practical help. First, they need help to understand just what their child's handicap is and how it will affect that child's development. This in part involves information. More importantly it means being helped to understand this information. The parents of a child with cystic fibrosis, when told that this is the diagnosis of its handicap, are not necessarily able to understand the implcations of this term either for their child or for themselves. The information given therefore needs to be personalized for their own situation – it needs to be given a context in terms of the actual life those particular parents lead. One mistake a number of helping organizations make is to provide a whole body of information at one time. Many parents find this both overwhelming and worrying. What may be more useful, according to some, is to have the information provided at a variety of points in the child's development so that they can set meaningful targets for their child's behaviour and assess its progress more accurately.

A second need that many parents express when confronted with the fact of a handicapped child is for contact with the parents of children with the same handicap. This is an important need, not only in terms of practical information and advice (especially important for the parents of a child with a physical handicap), but also in terms of the social support for the parents. Whilst the community often finds children with physical and mental handicap difficult to cope with, the parents of other handicapped children do provide at least one group who are supportive. Quite a number of parents report that, after a while, they are able to cope better with their handicapped child than with the reactions of strangers (and sometimes friends and relatives) to their child. Other parents of handicapped children often provide the necessary support for coping with their child in the community in which they live.

The final need which parents have, and one which is very practical, concerns a full and clear knowledge of their rights to benefits and allowances provided by the community in which they live. In every country which offers support to parents of handicapped children, the rate of take up of available benefits is less than the number of people entitled to these benefits. Whilst some do not need the benefits because of their financial status, others fail to claim through their ignorance of the available resources. These resources are many and varied, and differ from area to area, country to country. But they are generally intended to give direct assistance to the child and to the parents.

These are not the only practical needs which parents have. Other needs include help with the child at certain times, the need for a rest from the child through a holiday or an evening out and the ability to share the burden of coping with the practical tasks of coping with another person, at least for a time.

But the emotional needs of the parents of a handicapped child, whatever order they are placed in by the helper, are important. If left unmet, they impair the parents' ability to cope with the more obvious practical needs of their child.

One problem which the parents of a handicapped child sometimes face when being helped by professional helpers or para-professional volunteers concerns the ways in which these helpers interpret their feelings. For example, many descriptions of parents use emotionally charged terms such as 'guilt', 'shame', 'hostility' or 'remorse', as if the meaning of these terms was self-evident. Some helpers, for example, believe that guilt is felt, despite their obvious love of their child, because the parents have a deep-seated desire to reject their child; others see this guilt as being connected to the parents' feelings that they cannot express enough love for their child. Similarly, the parent who expresses an interest in the child's education is seen as being excessively concerned about the child and regarded as projecting his or her own guilt onto the work of the teacher; whereas the parent who expresses little interest in his or her child's education is seen as trying to repress feelings of guilt. Such interpretations ensure that the parents cannot win when faced with the vocabulary of motives employed by their 'helpers'.

To show how damaging such helper interpretations can be, here is an extract from a well-known writer on handicap who specifically addresses these remarks to social workers:

> . . . there is a grave risk that the parents' relationship with the child will be disturbed. If they become aware of their feelings of guilt, they very often over-protect their child. On the one hand this often hinders his development by creating an unnecessary degree of dependency; on the other hand they make quite exorbitant sacrifices, often at the expense of their own mental health and sometimes that of the other children. If they are unable to face their guilt they may simply reject the child, withdrawing their affections from him, whether or not they reject him physically. Some parents assume that their handicapped child is incapable of any development so they fail to give him the stimulation which he needs to use his limited capacities to the full; others may refuse to accept the diagnosis and drag him from one expert to another in search of some magical cure, while at the same time they may discourage him from doing what he can by being never satisfied with his achievements and always demanding something more.

(Heimler, 1979, p. 52)

This makes it impossible for the parents to be 'normal' – any expression of interest, feeling or lack of feeling has an interpretation which comes back to the parents' guilt. Whatever the parent does or feels can be understood only in terms of this writer's own reasoning. What such interpretations do is make grieving for loss and coping with handicap much more difficult to achieve. More important than offering interpretations to parents is the task of the helper in facilitating the release of emotions so that painful feelings can be faced and can be accepted. Such rationalizations of complex emotions, ending in the labelling of any parent behaviour as 'a problem', also make it more difficult for the parents to know what to do to help their child's development – they do not know what objectives to set for their child or how to show their feelings towards their child – whatever they do is 'pathological'.

What happens when helpers seek to interpret parents' thoughts, feelings and behaviour in this way is that the helper confirms his own thoughts and feelings about the parents' situation rather than hears the thoughts and feelings from their points of view. As one parent said when interviewed by a researcher, the helpers she had seen had 'got this training but they don't really know how you feel' (Fox, 1974). The helper's task is primarily to facilitate the parents' understanding of their own feelings, thoughts and behaviour in terms and ways which are meaningful to them, given their own biographies and experience. For handicap is not simply an objective phenomenon – the way in which parents think and feel and the way in which others (helpers included) react help to shape the nature of the handicap and the way in which individuals cope with it.

In a number of studies, Booth (1978) documents the way in which parents of handicapped children seek to cope with the fact of handicap. He shows that many of the coping strategies and tactics adopted by parents conflict with the strategies and tactics preferred by professional helpers. One common coping strategy adopted by parents (especially those who are parents of physically handicapped children) is called 'normalization' – the child is treated as they would treat any normal child. 'He's just like the rest of us' or 'he's the same as I was at his age' are two kinds of expressions of this strategy. But professional helpers often feel that this coping strategy indicates that the parents are 'unable to face reality'. Yet the reality for them is that they are able – or feel able – to treat their child as normal. A second coping strategy adopted by some parents is almost the exact opposite of 'normalization' – we shall call it 'protection'. Those parents who use the protection strategy seek to shelter the handicapped child from the hazards of life, ensuring that their needs are regularly assessed and met and equipping them so as to minimize contact with the world of the normal child. Many doctors and social workers label this strategy as 'over-protective' and they suggest that the parents have some inability to face up to painful feelings. Yet these parents find that this strategy is effective for them. A third coping strategy involves the parents in accepting that their child is handicapped but denying that this handicap unduly affects their family life – 'whilst Mike is crippled, we live just like any ordinary family'. Many social workers and doctors regard this reaction as unacceptable, suggesting that the parents are ignoring some very real effects upon their family life-style.

Rather than finding ways to criticize these particular strategies, the helper's task is to encourage and enable the parents of a handicapped child to use the coping strategy that best suits them. Whatever the strategy, it is acceptable. The helper needs to help them to develop the tactics which will enable the strategy to work.

Conclusion

This chapter has made a number of points concerning both the nature of the reactions of parents to the fact of handicap and the way in which they cope with this fact. It is clear that: (a) the crisis of handicap is a recurrent one for the parents of a handicapped child – it is not surprising that divorce rates are high amongst families affected by handicap; (b) the crisis for parents is not only emotional – practical and financial issues are involved too; (c) the emotional reactions of parents are best characterized in terms of grief work – parents need to avoid being trapped by the labels which some professional and para-professional helpers wish to attach to them.

One surprising feature of the community response to handicap is that there is a general lack of counselling facilities for the parents of handicapped children. Many parents of handicapped children are now developing self-help and mutual aid groups to give practical guidance and counselling to each other. The development of such self-help activity is important, not simply because it provides an effective form of social support, but also because it provides a ready-made group which can take up an advocacy role on behalf of children with a particular handicap and their parents.

CHAPTER 8

UNEMPLOYMENT – THE PERSON AND THE FAMILY

Introduction

Unemployment and job-loss are serious problems affecting many millions of persons in the developed world. Young people who leave formal education and are then without work; men and women of all ages, skills and experience who find themselves as job-losers after a period of working which varies from between a few days to a life-time – all can be significantly affected by being unemployed.

In this chapter, we focus upon the impact of unemployment for those for whom the experience of being without work is a crisis. Many of those who are unemployed are unemployed only for temporary periods. Though many of these will experience this transition from one job to another as a crisis, many find effective ways of coping. More serious, in our experience of working with unemployed adults and young people, are the reactions of those who are long-term unemployed. This group – which includes people of all abilities and skills – experience serious emotional, physical and practical consequences of unemployment which can be debilitating. Also clear is the impact of unemployment upon the family. We shall document here some research work by Stephen Murgatroyd and Michael Shooter of the Coping with Crisis Research Group at the Open University showing the reactions of non-coping families to the presence of a long-term unemployed family member, for this research suggests particular actions for those who wish to help families affected by unemployment.

Before describing the impact of unemployment upon the person and the family it is necessary to caution those who seek to help. Unemployment is essentially a political and economic problem. Helping individuals come to terms with their reactions, developing strategies and tactics for coping with unemployment and working with organizations to provide mutual aid and self-help for the unemployed are necessary tasks for those with a helping commitment. But they will not remove the problem of unemployment – ironically, it may make it easier for companies and governments to sanction more unemployment. Providing assistance programmes and counselling to young unemployed persons will not create jobs. Helpers need to ensure that their work does not become a part of the problem for unemployed people rather than a part of the solution. They can act as advocates for unemployed individuals or groups; they can help individuals or groups increase their command over social resources, so that they can increase their opportunities for work; they can bring to the attention of politicians and investors the impact of unemployment upon the family and the individuals within it. What they need to avoid becoming is an excuse for unemployment. Effective counselling and advocacy could lead some employers to feel that workers would be 'just as well off without work'. Whilst a small minority (mainly the higher paid worker) might be, most do not feel so.

The Physical Impact of Unemployment

The effects of job-loss upon physical health and well-being have been well documented. Sidney Cobb and Stanislav Kasl (1977), in a thorough investigation, have suggested that these effects include an increased risk of coronary failure, an increase in the likelihood of the person becoming arthritic or diabetic and an increase in their susceptibility to gout, hypertension and peptic ulcers. Further studies also suggest that the stress-related features of unemployment have led to a higher incidence of alcoholism amongst unemployed workers (Jacobson and Lindsay, 1979; Smart, 1979), despite the fact that their economic position severely reduces the size of their income.

Though these physical effects are important, it is clear that unemployment and job-loss have psychological effects too. Whilst the psychological studies concerned with unemployment do not appear as rigorous as those reported by Cobb and his co-workers, it seems clear that job-loss leads to a loss of self-esteem (Komarovsky, 1940; Tausky and Piedmont, 1967), to feeling inferior (Eisenberg and Lazarsfeld, 1938) and to a lowering of morale (Jahoda et al., 1970; Gould and Keynon, 1972) for those who face the prospect of a period without employment. For those who face a prolonged period of unemployment (a year or more) it may be the case that they experience acute psychological distress (Israeli, 1935). It is interesting to note the difference between these psychological effects and the physical effects as described in the available literature. The physical effects are specific symptoms which have disease or illness consequences, whereas the psychological features are generalized and unspecific.

Yet these physical and psychological features are linked: they are all stress-related reactions to the experience of becoming unemployed.

This suggests two tasks for those who wish to help the person. The first is to maintain the person's physical fitness through exercise and careful diet. Often this means replacing the physical exercise a person obtained through work (even office work can involve a lot of physical energy) with more systematic 'physical training' activities – yoga, jogging, a particular sport, swimming etc. The diet is also important, but may be more difficult to achieve since the person's purchasing power is affected by their changed job-status and this may make the purchase of necessary food more difficult. The second task for a helper is to reduce the experience of stress – several techniques for achieving this are suggested in Chapter 11. In pursuing this latter task, the helper needs to be aware of the emotional and personal significance of becoming unemployed.

Becoming Unemployed

According to Dennis Marsden and Euan Duff, employment brings a number of certainties to a person's experience. It provides him with a structure within which he can pace his life; it provides a beginning, a middle and an end to each day; it provides him with a structure within which he can plan his life, since work determines such things as the extent of leisure, the frequency of holidays, the consequences of illness for income and the level at which expectations for living standards can be set. In addition, work provides a status to the person: it establishes his 'occupation' and his role in relation to the community. In short, work has become a contract between the person and the community.

Job-loss breaks this contract. It leaves the person in limbo, unsure of his status and uncertain about his role. It leaves him shapeless – uncertain about the beginning, middle and end of each day, week or month. It leaves him bored – each day not only looks the same but feels the same. It leaves him poor – savings and benefit do not replace the spending power of a wage or salary. It leaves him isolated – he no longer has the free association he experienced with his workmates and he no longer has the income to make free association a matter of routine. Contrary to many views, unemployed persons have little leisure – they do not have sufficient funds to travel and then participate in many leisure activities. Within their families, the status of the unemployed changes. No longer are they able to provide support to others financially and they often feel that they are more of a 'burden' than an asset within the family. The full range of these experiences has the self-esteem consequences already referred to and often leads to a degree of depersonalization. Marsden and Duff cite many cases in which persons and their families are so affected by these features that all concerned experience a lowering of self-esteem and a degree of depersonalization and depression.

It is not surprising, therefore, that several studies of unemployment suggest that its effects are moderated by the degree of social support a person receives. Indeed, some studies have gone as far as to suggest that, given the right degree of support and a real prospect of future employment, job-loss can be viewed positively (see Little, 1976). Schlossberg and Leibowitz (1980), reviewing these studies, produce a typology of the person best able to cope with job-loss. Their typology includes such features as: (a) intimate family relationships; (b) a wide network of friends; (c) institutional support in the form of workshops offering basic coping skills training, job-searching help and adequate severance pay; and finally, (d) psychosocial competence, a positive coping orientation and positive experience of previous transitional life-events. Our experience would suggest that such people are rare.

More common are those who experience job-loss as a form of separation, with all the associated forms of attachment loss and grief work which has come, following Bowlby, to be associated with such separations. The pattern of job-loss–grieving which we have seen many times is similar to the pattern of grief work to be described in Chapter 9 (see pages 105 to 119). Here this same model is altered only to make it directly relevant to the experience of unemployment. The model in Chapter 9 is a more generalized grief-work model.

1 Loss – whether the job-loss has been anticipated or not, the first experience our clients typically report is the sense of loss, both in terms of loss of activity and in terms of loss of security. As one middle-aged ex-personnal manager said, 'it's as if I had lost a limb – it has changed what I do, how I am and how others see me. . . . I feel disabled, just as much as if I had lost a limb.'

2 Searching – The feeling of loss soon merges into the task of searching. Most researchers and observers have focused upon job-searching activities as the typical feature of this stage, but other search activities are also engaged at this point. These include such searches as 'for the real me' (an identity search), 'for the me I would really like to be' (a fantasy search) and for new means of survival (a survival search). Not all of these searching activities are fruitful in the sense that they are intended to lead to definite outcomes. All searching activities engaged in are, however, intended to lead to changes in self-thoughts and self-esteem. They are about trying to engage in some positive activity, irrespective of the actual outcome of that activity.

3 Re-finding – After a period of searching, described briefly above, the person enters a period of action in which it seems as if he has found some purposeful work. This may be work around the house – 'doing all those little jobs that needed doing, but which I could never get around to whilst I was in work . . .' – or may be work in the black economy. Most typically, the re-found activity is a poor and short-term substitute for paid employment and its positive effects are soon lost.

4 Re-loss – The loss of purpose from the re-found activities leads to a difficult stage in the job-loss–grief process and it is at this point that a number of critical physical and psychological effects are most frequently reported. These effects include some or all of the following: (a) denial of the consequences of being unemployed – frequently associated with alcoholism; (b) withdrawal from the reality of the situation, often leading to agitated depression and physical illness; (c) the development of learned helplessness; (d) freezing of both affect and consequent action, so that the person immunizes himself against *any* feelings and minimizes the extent to which he takes action which may affect (positively or negatively) the situation in which he finds himself; (e) hostility, especially towards others in the family and towards those in work; and finally (f) the development of grief and atonement feelings, which often show themselves in obsessive behaviours unlikely to lead to a resolution of the underlying cause of the condition, namely the lack of paid employment.

It is likely that the person will move between the stages of re-finding and re-loss with some regularity and that this 'reversal' between these two stages will continue either until a job is found or until the person is helped towards more adaptive responses to his situation.

5 Awareness – Following a period of grief work, described above, the person can be helped (by family, by others or through his own efforts) to understand more readily his condition. That is, he can develop a frame of thinking and feeling which better equips him to cope with the feelings and conditions which he now experiences and which helps to direct his opportunity awareness, self-awareness, transition learning and job-search activities into more positive and self-productive areas.

6 Burial – This final stage of the job-loss–grieving process which we have witnessed involves the person 'putting to rest' that version of himself losswith which he began the process. Following cathartic experiences, the person feels better able to cope and to help others to cope with the situation as it is. In short, the person is better able to maintain, develop and initiate relationships whilst at the same time coping with his own situation. As one middle-aged woman expressed it, 'I've found a box for my old self and I'm putting it away – I can now begin to move forward and see that my being out of work isn't my fault and that there are things I can do which are going to be helpful to me and others. . . . I've become a better person.'

This model of job-loss–grieving is an elaborate one, reflecting the experiences of a great many people. It seeks to reflect the dynamic quality of the process of 'becoming unemployed' and to highlight the intense nature of the emotional experience felt by the person put in this position. As counsellors and therapists, it is difficult for us to tackle the underlying cause of our client's problem: this is more rightly a task for industrialists, politicians and investors. Seeing unemployment experiences in the terms outlined here has, however, helped us more fully understand the frustrations and experiences of the increasing number of unemployed persons seeking our help.

This model suggests that the task of the helper is to facilitate grief work – a task frequently encountered in the accounts of crises provided in this text. But this is made more difficult by the stress which the person experiences, because of social isolation, lack of structure and relative poverty. Indeed, there are two central depressions seen in most of the unemployed persons for whom we have acted as counsellors. The first is the depression that arises from their grief at the loss of their job; the second is their depression which arises from the stress they are experiencing as an unemployed person living in relative poverty. These depressions feed on each other and can be made more complex by physical conditions. It is not enough, therefore, for the helper to focus upon the purely emotional reactions to unemployment. They need also to give attention to the unemployed person's physical needs (diet and fitness, warmth and shelter) and their practical needs (money, clothing, social support). Since some stress arises from these needs, they are not to be disregarded in favour of the more challenging emotional reactions.

Youth Unemployment

There are some important differences between the experience of un-employment for a person who has never been in work and the experience of job-loss. Two in particular are important.

First, the young person who experiences unemployment grieves not so much for the loss of a job but for the lack of opportunity to enter paid work. Many young people regard schooling as a preparation for work; they regard their age as equipping them for work and regard work as an essential element of their lives. Without work they have little money and are dependent upon their family for income. Without work their status is still that of a school pupil or student – a status that is unattractive to many organizations, clubs and individuals. Work establishes them in their contract with the community. Their failure to obtain work, through no fault of their own, leads to a grieving for the loss of an ideal and a depression arising from the collapse of an expectation. Some young people develop a lack of confidence in their general ability to predict events and in their social skills as a result of this depression.

Second, leaving school or education and going to work is a major event in the young person's relationship with his or her family. Psychologists call this a 'separation-individuation' event because it involves the young person achieving a new identity which is separate from that of the family. Such separation-individuation events are not easily achieved even when the young person is able to find work. The young person often fears being abandoned in the adult world – the fear of being 'an innocent abroad'. The parents of this young person often fear rejection by their 'child' once he enters the world of work. Normally, both these fears are offset by the hope of success at work and by the feeling of security the transition from education to work often releases. The denial of this hope and the failure of the young person to achieve security gives rise to a further source of potential crisis – namely a crisis due to the failure of the young person to achieve separation-individuation at the time when he and his parents were psychologically prepared for it.

The failure of a young person to obtain employment can significantly affect the dynamics of the family, causing distress to mother, father and other family members. The young person often takes the blame upon himself for the failure to obtain employment, often despite the fact that some several hundred young people in adjacent streets, towns, villages and cities are also without work simply because there are not enough vacancies for the number of job-seekers. Parents sometimes encourage this self-blame and the self-doubt to which it gives rise, since they are unable to accept that 'their child' should be unemployed when other young people are in work. Young people typically report tension at home, a lack of concern for their emotional well-being and an over-emphasis on finding a job when there are few to be found. These kinds of reactions create many situations for angry scenes and for the young person and other family members to feel distressed.

A major task for helpers engaged in work with young people involves working directly with the family to help them understand their son's or daughter's situation from their point of view (i.e., to develop a more empathic understanding) and to encourage them to accept and work within the limitations of their current social situation whilst at the same time engaging them in the task of changing that situation so that it might benefit their son or daughter and others. This sounds straightforward when expressed in this way. But it is difficult to achieve. In part this is because the information parents need to understand the situation their young person finds himself in is difficult to obtain and understand; in part this is because having an unemployed young person in the family is, to many, an indication of their failure to be successful as parents. A lot of emotional barriers have often to be dismantled before parents and other family members can begin to understand and accept the situation in which their own son or daughter finds himself.

Family Reactions to Unemployment

Stephen Murgatroyd and Michael Shooter have been examining the impact of unemployemnt on the structure of families as part of a larger study of crisis situations. They suggest that long-term unemployment in most families is coped with through active grief work at the loss of unemployment and by an honest sharing between family members of the feelings and thoughts that they experience. In addition, other studies show that coping families tend to be those which take immediate action to adjust to their new financial and social situation (Hayes and Nutman, 1980). For some, unemployment (especially when accompanied by reasonable severance pay) can be a productive transition event, providing them and their family with the opportunity for a significant change in many aspects of their lives – changes which have been inhibited by the fact of being 'in work'. The importance of Murgatroyd's and Shooter's work lies, however, in their observations of non-coping families and of the crises to which their failure to cope with the fact of unemployment give rise.

Murgatroyd and Shooter suggest that non-coping families affected by unemployment generally adopt one of two strategies. The first they call 'isolation'. This takes one of two forms. In the first form the family helps the unemployed person through the initial stages of grieving, but then isolates that person within the family and discourages further grief work. This often means that the person is 'stuck' in their grieving, reversing constantly between searching, re-finding and re-loss. Isolation is achieved by individuals within the family not being willing to listen and work through the grief of job-loss and by the unemployed person being labelled as 'not being able to cope'. In the second form of isolation, far more common in the work reported by Murgatroyd and Shooter, the family reacts to unemployment of a key member (especially the breadwinner) by collapsing – rebuilding around a new 'leader' in such a way as to isolate the unemployed person. This needs some explanation. Families typically interact in similar ways over time. Though family interactions differ between families, they are similar within the same family over time. When a significant change occurs – such as that arising from the death of a member or a significant change in the status of the member – then the typical interactions of that family also undergo change. The collapse referred to here is the collapse of these 'normal' patterns of interaction. The rebuilding is of new patterns of interaction without the unemployed person. Not only does the unemployed person figure less in the interaction patterns of the family, his or her needs and wants are regarded as marginal to the needs and wants which the family is willing to meet.

The second strategy adopted by the non-coping families studied by Murgatroyd and Shooter they call 'freezing'. In this strategy the family works hard at maintaining the life-style and pattern of its interactions as if nothing had happened to change the status of one of its members. To maintain this status-quo position it is necessary, as Murgatroyd and

Shooter point out, for the family to freeze its relationships not as they were before the affected person became unemployed but in the image of how they thought they should have been at that time. In other words, the family freezes itself in its ideal model for a family, given the circumstances in which they found themselves before job-loss was experienced. These two writers suggest that this strategy – more accurately described as 'idealized freezing' – is the strategy most common amongst non-coping families.

These two strategies suggest a difficult role for a helper. For not only do the family need to be enabled to cope with the reality of their situation (financial and emotional), they also need to examine the implications of their attempts at coping both for the individual who is unemployed and for the family as a whole. Our experience of seeking to help families examine their coping strategies in these circumstances suggests to us how painful coping with crisis can be. What is more, many helpers find themselves faced with a personal crisis over the degree of confrontation they sometimes have to engage in and over the extent to which they are responsible for the emotional pain a particular person within the family experienced during the process of being helped.

Our experience also suggests that the family and individuals within it do not expect to grieve over the loss of a job or the failure of a young person to find work. When they experience the beginnings of mourning they feel that they are somehow over-reacting and that they are abnormal. A major task for a person seeking to help the individual or the family or both is to help them acknowledge the normality of job-loss grieving and to help them accept the naturalness of their depression. This is not an easy task for helpers primarily engaged in minimizing and reducing emotional pain, but it seems necessary in order to enable the family to cope more effectively with the fact of unemployment.

Conclusion

This chapter has examined the physical, personal and family reactions to unemployment and has given a special emphasis to the idea that job-loss most naturally leads to a form of grief work which the person and those close to him or her are best advised to work through. In giving emphasis to the psychological aspects of unemployment, it is not our intention to neglect the political and economic aspects of unemployment. As was stated at the beginning of this chapter, unemployment is essentially a political problem. Helping a person cope with the personal crisis this gives rise to does not contribute towards a political solution to the problem of unemployemnt as such – it helps only to alleviate personal suffering. Helpers need to be mindful of this political context when developing programmes of counselling and mutual aid.

CHAPTER 9

LOSS AND GRIEF

Introduction

This chapter is not about death or exclusively about bereavement. It is about loss – about the mourning that occurs when a limb or vital organ is removed by surgery or accident, about the grief work that is undertaken when a person who has been very close dies or when a person that mattered becomes so estranged as to be dead to us. An important finding of many studies of grieving and loss is that the process of grieving and the grief work that is identified with mourning is the same process that is used for other forms of loss. Whilst not all losses of limbs or deaths or estrangements constitute a crisis, they often do. This chapter seeks to document the grief work process and to show how a person might be helped through that process.

The term grief work has already occurred a number of times and will recur frequently in this chapter. We therefore need to explain it. The term was first used by Sigmund Freud as a description of the thoughts, feelings and actions of those most vulnerable following the death of a person that was close to them. In his book *Mourning and Melancholia*, Freud observed that people who had experienced a bereavement often thought and felt that the dead person was lost in some way and would return; that it was, in some way, their fault that the person had got lost and that they should act both in anticipation of his return and in a manner which showed and recognized their guilt. Some fifty years later, a pscyhologist specializing in the study of stress, I. L. Janis, coined the term 'worry work' as a description of the thinking, feeling and action that occurs in the anticipation of misfortune, crisis or personal disaster. Worry work is a device used by a person to focus attention upon possible dangers, upon his thoughts and feelings about his 'crisis' situation and upon his strategy and tactics for coping with this crisis.

Grief work differs from worry work in two important respects. First, and most obviously, worry work generally precedes a particular event or crisis whilst grief work refers specifically to loss and to the processes of grieving about that loss. Grief work is thus much more focused than the work of worry, involving specific processes. Though we shall not suggest that there is only one form of grief and that all grievers follow this one pattern, grief work does seem a much more systematic process than the work of worry, as we shall see below.

Whilst stressing the differences between grief work and the work of worry, this chapter has to deal with both of these forms of activity. This is for two reasons. First, some losses are anticipated. For example, surgical operations for the removal of a limb or a breast or death following a diagnosis of some terminal illness (i.e., leukemia, cancer, lassa-fever, rabies) are all anticipated in some way, even if only for a brief period. During this anticipatory period, worry work takes place. This worry work is undertaken both by the person anticipating their own losses and by the persons close to them. Secondly, worry work can of itself lead to loss – it is possible to die from a broken heart or to lose skills or senses through worry about them. Whilst they are different in nature, they are closely related processes that require exploration and study in any discussion of crises.

Four Cases

To illustrate a number of situations and experiences that involve grief work we begin with four cases. As with other materials in this book, these cases show that reactions to similar situations differ significantly between people and that the grieving process is common to many different loss-situations.

Mike is fifty-six. For many years he has worked as a scaffolder, erecting large scaffolding structures around historic buildings in order to aid and facilitate renovation work. Despite his considerable skills, he recently had a serious fall in which he broke both arms and completely shattered a leg. Indeed, so bad were the leg fractures that it was decided to amputate.

For almost six days after the amputation, Mike could still feel the presence of the leg. When he was beginning to be convinced that the leg had actually gone, he began to think that it might be possible for them to 'stick it back' – whilst he realized that this thought was irrational, it was a thought that recurred. When he eventually accepted that the leg was lost and that he would be fitted with a new leg, he began to be angry that he should have to suffer the indignity of an artificial leg and have to learn to walk again 'at my age'. It took about six months for Mike to adjust to his situation. During this time he fluctuated between coping and non-coping and experienced a period of depression, mainly about the loss of his job and the subsequent need for him to seek a new kind of employment.

The loss of his limb and of his job had serious effects on Michael, some of which are mentioned here (Chapter 8 looked at the experience of job-loss). But these reactions were not as strong as those experienced by Sheila at the loss of her daughter.

Sheila was thirty-two and had long wanted a baby. Though she had been pregnant before, she had lost her first baby. Her emotional investment in the second birth was substantial. The baby's birth was natural, and Sheila was especially proud of the fact that she had successfully used breathing exercises and relaxation training techniques as her only form of prophy-laxis during the period of her labour. Four hours after the birth, when Sheila was asleep, the baby died. No specific indication of the cause of death was ever discovered.

Wracked with emotional pain, Sheila's husband agreed to a cremation directly after the post-mortem. The baby was never given a name and neither parent attended the simple ceremony of the cremation nor did they ask to keep their child's ashes.

After an initial depression, which debilitated Sheila, the couple decided not to have further children. Sheila had a hysterectomy. The couple never talked about their two lost children. Marital and sexual relations became very strained and they both sought marriage guidance. The marriage guidance counsellor, in the eleventh week of their counselling contract, discovered the facts about their two children and worked with them to help them grieve at the loss of both of them. After twenty-five sessions (a total of forty-three hours), the couple began to live a more normal life and later adopted a girl.

Whilst the critical task with Sheila was to help her grieve the loss of her children so that she was enabled both to cope with her own feelings and her relationships with her husband, Mary's difficulties concerned her inability to stop grieving and return to a more normal pattern of working and living.

Mary was forty-seven and held a senior position in a government pension agency. Her husband, Frank, also worked in the same agency. She described their relationship as ideal and they were known locally as the happiest couple 'this side of the iron curtain'. They did so many things together because their hobbies, work and interests were so similar. What is more, their children were also loving and warm towards them.

Frank's sudden death from a coronary failure shocked Mary. Even a month after the funeral, she continued to prepare his lunch, to lay his table place, to lay out his clothes. She said 'I just don't think of him as being dead. . . . I think he's going to walk through that door at any moment.' She is clinically depressed and receiving chemo-therapeutic (drug) treatment for this depression. She is beginning to fear going out of the house – 'I have to be here in case he does come back. . . . It would be awful if he came back and found me out somewhere.' She has been rejecting of the help of others, especially her eldest daughter. Her daughter says that 'she's so confused, depressed and disoriented that I just don't know what she might do next'.

Eight months after Frank's death, Mary tried to commit suicide and was admitted as an emergency patient to a hospital. There she was seen by a psychiatrist, who reduced her drug-dependence and encouraged her to grieve in a more direct and a more focused way. Ten and a half months later, she is just beginning to return to the normal process of her life. As she says, she is 'picking up the pieces and trying to become Mary – single woman – again . . . and it's not easy'.

Mary's suicide could have been successful – she would have died because of a 'broken heart' and the shattering of her world. Jack's loss is not a human loss but the loss of an animal. His reactions to this loss are nonetheless as deep and as critical and serious for him as any of the losses described above.

Jack is sixty-eight and has never been married. Since retiring from his job as a toolmaker in a small engineering company which he joined at the age of twenty-two, his constant companion has been a labrador called 'Nixon'. He called it Nixon, he used to tell friends, 'because I never knew what trick he was going to get up to next'. Jack had owned Nixon for fifteen years and had often ensured that his dog had more comfort and better food than himself. Jack boasted that he was fitter now than he'd been before he owned the dog – the exercise of walking the dog and of ensuring its fitness ensured the fitness of both of them. Nixon went everywhere with Jack and if Nixon was not allowed into certain buildings then Jack would not go into them either.

Nixon was killed one day as he ran across the road to chase after another dog. Jack saw the accident, but was helpless to prevent it. He said afterwards, 'One moment I was smiling at the audacity of the dog, chasing after a Yorkshire Terrier, and the next I was weeping like a six-month-old baby as a car took the life out of its lungs.'

Jack reacted as if the loss had been that of a wife. He refused to leave the house for several days and became very depressed. He ate very little and slept fitfully. He refused offers of help, saying that all he wanted was 'my Nixon back' and for 'somebody to do that bloody motorist'. It was three and a half months before Jack was seen regularly out and about. His formerly outgoing persona had changed to one of melancholy and he was bitter about everything – motorists, foreigners, prices, the weather. He became very prone to illness and forgetful. He died almost exactly twelve months after the death of Nixon.

A neighbour said of this six months that 'it was as if Jack had lost his purpose in living – it's amazing just how attached a person can become to a dog.'

No special claim is being made about these cases. They are neither unusual nor typical. They reflect a range of situations in which loss is experienced and a range of reactions which relate to grief work, as we shall describe it below. One point to note about all of these cases, and the others that will be used in this chapter, is the intensity of the feeling associated with loss. Whilst the period of time between loss and reshaping of the mourner's life can vary considerably, the intensity of that experience seems especially powerful. What is also clear is that reactions to loss affect many aspects of a person's life, not just his feelings about the lost person, lost animal, lost skill or feature. Loss can affect intellectual processes (Jack's memory was affected), interpersonal relations (Jack and Sheila's relationships with others suffered as a result of their loss), beliefs, attitudes, emotions and physical well-being. Grief work is painful.

Society and Loss

Because grief work is painful and distressing, the reaction of society to a distressed and grieving person can critically affect the extent and success of grieving. Since death is a very public event – usually involving legal formalities, funerals, press announcements and a number of relatives – and an event which most people will witness in some way and all will experience, it is surprising that death is so rarely talked about and discussed. The implications of surgical or accidental loss of a limb or a crucial organ are rarely discussed until it is certain that the issues are real for that person, and even then the focus is more upon practical issues than upon feelings, anxieties and thoughts about self.

In *Helping The Troubled Child*, Stephen Murgatroyd documents some of the social values which lead to and encourage this reluctance to examine the emotional implications of circumstances. These values include the emphasis upon achievement, upon conforming to a stereotype of 'happy and contented' person, dealing with personal difficulties by 'grinning and bearing it' in the belief that 'time will heal' or that 'you can't have everything your own way all the time'. More significantly, there is an implicit assumption that unfortunate things should not happen to someone and, if they do, then the person must be in part to blame. The fact that loss by death is inevitable – friends and relatives will die – and that death is an inevitability which needs to be understood and accepted is not generally the basis of certain actions and reactions at the time a death actually occurs. Indeed, some writers have noted that the portrayal of death through violence on television in both fiction and fact has obscured the fact that death is peaceful for a majority and inevitable for all.

Others have noted the strange way in which death in particular is viewed by society. Margaret Mead, a notable observer of social life, noted that 'we celebrate birth and a wedding and then pretend that there is no death'. Elton McNeil, in a more outspoken comment, suggests that 'our culture has sanitized and denied death as a way of life'. That these observations contain more than a grain of truth is clear from the way in which death is now institutionalized by undertakers (who have recently begun to call themselves bereavement counsellors), the Church and the State. It is possible for a person to die and for the body never to be seen by the majority of those most affected by the death. The slickness of modern funeral services and church services increases the sense of unreality many experience when thinking about death or when recalling experiences of coping with the death of a close friend of relative. Though efficient, the way in which society currently handles the dead does not encourage grieving: in fact, in increases the mourner's chance of denying that the death is a real event.

Sarah Morris, in a useful book called *Grief – How To Live With It*

(Morris, 1981), notes too that the level of social support for those who have been bereaved is declining. She suggests that there has been a decline of the investment of emotional energy by the clergy of many denominations, and noted the reluctance of the family as a whole to share in the process of greiving and of the failure of educational institutions to enable and encourage children and young adults to consider death and their thoughts and feelings about it. She observes, from her own experience, that even friends are unsure whether to help or whether they are best advised to leave the mourning person alone. In other parts of this book (see especially pages 163 to 167) the value of social support for coping with crisis will be stressed – a whole chapter is devoted to this later in the book. If social support is declining for those who need to cope with death, then it is more difficult for many to cope with the experience of grief work.

Just as death is difficult for many to talk about and is socially not a sanctioned subject, so too is disfigurement and loss of limbs, breasts or facilities difficult to discuss and share in our society. The loss of limbs is thought to have effects on the bodily abilities of the person over and above those actually experienced. The loss of a breast is seen as an ending to sexuality and feminism, though the majority of women who experience masectomy lead normal lives after the operation. It is not only the traumatic operation leading to changes in the body-image and body-function of the person that is not socially sanctioned talk. Rarely do discussions about ageing take place. The idea that age brings with it considerable physical deterioration (which is not generally true) is accepted by most so as to avoid discussion about the personal responsibility we each have towards our own bodies. All of these kinds of issues and experiences are thought to be so intensely personal and private that the discussion of them or sharing concerns about their possibility is an intrusion into a person's privacy.

A later section of this chapter will document some of the ways in which a grieving person can be helped by others. What is important to note here is that both the person engaged in grief work and those seeking to enable that person complete their grief work often find themselves working alone because society is generally not supportive of the self-disclosure and pain involved. As one husband remarked shortly after the death of his wife, 'I cried once at work . . . everyone just left me alone and what I wanted was just one person to share something with and they all walked away . . . they couldn't cope with my grief.'

The Grief Work Process

There are a variety of descriptions of grief work available. The most complete is provided by John Bowlby in his book on attachment and loss (Bowlby, 1973). We have chosen to offer a description of grief work as a six-stage process. Not all of these stages will be experienced by those facing a loss. Not all will experience these stages in this sequence. Some may even be relieved at the loss of another person or at the loss of a hitherto painful body organ.

These, then, are the six stages of grieving as we have seen them. As stated throughout this chapter, this model can be useful as a description of a person's reactions to a variety of losses – indeed you will already have come across this model in Chapter 8.

1 Loss – Whether the loss has been anticipated or not, the first experience people typically report is the sense of loss, in terms of affection and familiarity, in terms of expectancy and in terms of security. As one person who had lost a limb said, 'You'll never know how, in the first few hours, I just couldn't get used to the fact that what I had always known about my body was no longer true.'

2 Searching – The feeling of loss soon merges into the task of searching. Most researchers and observers have focused upon activities such as searching for the lost person or searching for the lost limb or body-organ or skill as the typical feature of this stage, but other search activities are also engaged at this point. These include such searches as 'for the real me' (an identity search), 'for the me I would really like to be' (a fantasy search) and for the new means of survival (a survival search). Not all of these searching activities are fruitful in the sense that they are intended to lead to definite outcomes. All searching activities engaged in are, however, intended to lead to changes in self-thoughts and self-esteem. They are about trying to engage in some positive activity, irrespective of the actual outcome of that activity.

3 Re-finding – After a period of searching, described briefly above, the person enters a period of action in which it seems as if he has found that which he has lost, be it a person or a body-organ. Sometimes this re-finding is purely in the imagination. A person who has lost sight in one eye sometimes imagines that he has re-gained this lost sight. Sometimes this re-finding takes the form of finding a replacement which is thought to be 'just like' that which has been lost. The loss of

someone close is often dealt with by finding someone else who substitutes for that person, almost as if the new person was the other re-found.

4 Re-loss – The realization that the re-found person is not the original or that the re-found organ or sense or skill or limb is not actually there leads to a difficult stage in the loss-grief process and it is at this point that a number of critical physical and psychological effects are most frequently reported. These effects include some or all of the following: (a) denial of the consequences of having experienced a loss – frequently used as a trigger for drinking in excess; (b) withdrawal from the reality of the situation, often leading to agitated depression and physical illness; (c) the development of a feeling of being helpless and acting helpless; (d) freezing of both affect and consequent action, so that the person immunizes himself against any feelings and minimizes the extent to which he takes action which may affect (positively or negatively) the situation in which he finds himself; (e) hostility, especially towards others in the family and towards those trying to befriend and to be helpful; and finally (f) the development of grief and atonement feelings, which often show themselves in obsessive behaviours unlikely to lead to a resolution of the underlying cause of the condition, namely the permanent loss of a person or body-organ.

It is likely that the person will move between the stages of re-finding and re-loss with some regularity and that this 'reversal' between these two stages will continue until the person is helped towards more adaptive responses to his situation. It is this reversal between these two stages that most vividly resembles the grief work so clearly described by Colin Murray Parkes.

5 Awareness – Following a period of grief work, described briefly above, the person can be helped (by family, by others or through his own efforts) to understand more readily his condition. That is, the person can develop a frame of thinking and feeling which better equips him to cope with the feelings and conditions which he now experiences and which helps to direct his opportunity awareness, self-awareness, transition learning and self-searching activities into more positive and self-productive areas. It should be stressed, however, that this stage does not mean that the person is able to resolve the inner conflicts which are characteristic of the grief work undertaken at the previous stage. Essentially, the person puts himself or is helped by others to put himself

back in touch with his own situation and is helped to better use his own repertoire of coping strategies and tactics.

6 Burial – This final stage of the loss–grieving process which we have witnessed involves the person 'putting to rest' that version of himself with which he began the process. Following attempts to come to terms with his loss and the experience of working in the awareness phase, the person feels better able to cope and to help others to cope with the situation as it is. In short, the person is better able to maintain, develop and initiate relationships whilst at the same time coping with his own situation. As one middle-aged woman expressed it, 'I've found a box for my old self and I'm putting it away – I can now begin to move forward and see that my being a widow isn't my fault and that there are things I can do which are going to be helpful to me and others. . . . I've become a new person.'

It should be clear that grief work is painful and sometimes distressing. It can involve some physical symptoms – tiredness, lack of sleep, irregular eating, aches and pains, headaches and stomach cramps, stomach upsets – and these must not be too readily put down as 'psychosomatic'. Whatever the cause of the physical symptoms, they are nonetheless often actually present. More often, the reactions to loss involve disorganization and disorientation – the person is less able to cope, to focus upon specific issues, to communicate.

Wendy, who had lost her husband when only twenty-three, kept a diary in which she recorded her feelings from shortly after being told of her husband's death in a work accident until she felt 'normal again'. The adjectives she used to describe her feelings during this eighteen-month period were as follows: sorrow, anguish, pain, weepy, disbelief, despair, anxious, lonely, frustrated, guilty, regretful, resentful, bitter, empty, numbness, yearning, loving, changing, mellowing, experiencing, knowing, remembering. She said of the experience of grief work that 'I've never felt so many emotions just flooding over me – they were so strong, and changing all the time. People tried to help, but it was difficult for me to explain how I felt since I hadn't really felt that way before. I was shocked at first, then I didn't know what I was doing. Gradually, I let my feelings come up and I worked and worked at them as they arrived, but it has meant that I've had to change not only because I have lost my husband but also because I know more about myself.'

The model we present suggests that resolution of grief through burial is an inevitable consequence of passing through these six stages. But this is not the case. Many people do not arrive at the fifth and sixth stages – they get 'stuck' in the reversal between re-finding and re-loss, continually finding and losing substitutes for the real thing. Alternatively they deny that the loss has consequences for them and do not get past the first stage. Others delay their grief work by burying themselves in work, in sorting out their affairs, in physical activity and only later permit themselves a modicum of grief. Some exaggerate their grief at stages one and two so much so that they begin to use grief as a fantasy for achieving comfort and help from others. A considerable number stop grieving by feeling guilty, using phrases like 'If only I . . .' or 'I should have . . . and then . . .' to tell themselves it was their fault. Others use drugs – prescribed by doctors or alcohol or illegal drugs – to deaden the experience of grieving. The model is therefore a model of the ideal grieving person – one who works through grief and comes to terms with the experience of loss.

Helping the Grieving Person

Those helping a person cope with loss have a number of difficulties. The first and most important one is time. The grief work process outlined here can take a considerable period – sometimes up to two years. Though some cope with loss much more quickly (within five–seven months), the time commitment a helper might need to engage in could be significant. The second concerns the intensity of the emotional experience that grief work usually is. Helpers need to be able to cope themselves with significant emotional discharges across a variety of emotions, as the descriptions of Wendy's experience above shows. A third difficulty, already mentioned, is the reaction of society to loss – especially death. The pressure not to grieve at a loss is considerable and affects not only the grieving person but also those seeking to help the person grieve. The final problem is how to help the grieving person.

There are three things helpers should avoid doing. The first is taking responsibility for the grieving person's life. Whilst the shock and disorientation of a particular loss may be considerable, the person still needs to function and operate effectively in the real world. They will not be helped in doing this if others are taking the responsibility for their 'real life', thus permitting them to spend more time in their fantasy world. The person needs to be enabled to grieve. He also needs to be able to operate effectively in the real world.

A second 'don't' for helpers concerns tranquillisers. There is a temptation to deal with the pain of grieving by seeking to minimize it. Doctors prescribe drugs for this and many helpers seek to minimize pain by offering 'tranquillising' and comforting words aimed at stopping the discharge of emotion. Whilst some grieving persons need medical aid to cope with their grief (they should be encouraged to seek sound medical advice if this is the case), it is better to encourage people to work through their grief rather than deny it or postpone it.

The final 'don't' for helpers concerns the way in which they talk about the loss. When a child or husband has been lost, many family members stop referring to the lost person – they feel talking about them may lead to painful memories being evoked. This avoidance is a form of denial and it seeks to minimize the importance of the lost person in the life of the griever. If the lost person comes up in conversation naturally then it is natural to talk about that person. The same is true for lost body-organs or limbs. They were a significant part of the grieving person's life before they were lost – why deny this just because they have been lost?

A most significant need that grievers have when facing up to their grief work is for someone to be available, especially in the late afternoon and early evening. They need to know that, should they want to share their thoughts and feelings with another person, they are available to them. In the early period of grieving, this is especially important – many want this contact for three to four days immediately after the loss and regularly thereafter. Most often at these sessions, they need to be encouraged to discharge their emotions – to bring out in the open their thoughts and feelings. This involves the helper in both accepting that person as they are then (not in terms of what they used to be or might soon become) and in encouraging the person to regard their experience of grieving as being a normal reaction to the loss they have experienced. So many grieving persons do not think that their experience of grief can be normal – they assume that there must be something seriously wrong with them. A reassurance about the intensity of grieving and about the normative nature of the various phases of grieving is sometimes enough to aid grief work.

Critically, grieving persons need to be encouraged to accept their loss as a reality. They need to recognize that their loss is both real and permanent. No matter what replacements are found – artificial limbs or a new marriage partner – they will not be the same as that which has been lost. To help them, they need to know something about the reasons for the loss and the nature of the loss. They might need to talk to those who were involved with the loss – who were there or who tried to help. Acceptance is critical.

They also need to want to work through the experience, not only because it will enable them to come more effectively to terms with their loss but also to learn more about their own ability to cope with loss – something that might be helpful to them on other occasions. Whilst grief work is painful, it is a powerful learning opportunity.

Finally, the grieving persons need to want and be able to share honestly with other immediate family members their experience of the loss. In particular, children need to be involved in understanding and accepting the loss – they are capable of grieving and will need to grieve if the loss significantly affects them.

Anticipating Loss

Not all grief work has to be done following some unexpected event, such as an accident or a sudden death. Quite a number of people are able to anticipate their grief work since the loss itself is predictable. For example, a person with leukemia knows that he is going to die within a certain time; a person with a gangrenous leg knows that it is likely to be amputated; a person in hospital for a hysterectomy or a gall stone removal knows that he is to experience surgical loss. Anticipating loss involves the work of worry.

The work of worry, as we have already indicated, involves the active rehearsal of future events. The person doing the work of worry works through each potential source of stress and distress so as to examine possible courses of action, his thoughts and feelings and develop a coping strategy. This search for better coping is motivated by the anxiety engendered by the forthcoming loss. It is important for helpers to realize that it is the work rather than the worry that is the most important feature of worry work: individuals need to be helped to work through their stress and be discouraged from simply worrying. In particular, they need to engage in the discharge of negative emotions and actively to work through their thoughts and feelings about the forthcoming loss.

Earlier in this chapter some of the differences between worry work and grief work were briefly mentioned. It is important for helpers to recognize these differences. First, worry work is undertaken both by the person experiencing the loss (the 'loser') and by those with whom they are closely associated: in some situations which involve grief work (death or severe mental retardation, for example) the grieving is experienced only by those who are friends or relatives of the 'loser'. Second, worry work has a distinct end point – the loss itself; grief work can take many months and years to resolve itself. Helpers need to encourage the work of worry in the context of this firm end point. Third, the patterns of worry work and grief work are different. Whereas there are clear patterns in the grieving process, such patterns are not as clear for worry work. Further, there is some evidencs that the 'worrier' is more able to shape his worry work than he is able to shape grieving. By seeking to selectively avoid information, for example, worriers can minimize their anxiety. Alternatively, by actively seeking out information about the forthcoming loss and working through the implications of that information, the worrier can effectively develop coping strategies that will equip him for grieving. Finally, and this is a most important difference between worry work and grieving, the work of worry is generally accompanied by hope. The worrier thinks that the diagnosis may be wrong or that the prognosis is unduly pessimistic or that the surgery may prove unnecessary once the operation begins. Once the loss has occurred such hopes are lost too. The helper, whilst not belittling these hopes, needs to ensure that the hopes do not become so fantastic as to make the shock of loss greater – they need to minimize fantasy and maximize understanding.

Many who have written about anticipating loss suggest that 'good' anticipation (meaning that the work of worry enhances coping) will reduce both the intensity and severity of grieving. Most empirical evidence, however, suggests that the loss generally occurs before the work of worry is completed and that the loss itself still comes as a considerable shock to those most affected by it. Helpers need to be mindful of this in their work with individuals or families engaged in worry work. For it suggests the need to help them prepare for the grieving process as well as for the loss.

One other point needs to be made about anticipating loss. It is that, though much of the work of worry will concern thoughts and feelings, most losses involve some practical arrangements. For example, a death of an adult involves questions about who inherits goods; the loss of a limb involves questions about the physical arrangements for return from hospital; the loss of sight involves questions about physical arrangements and training. Sometimes these practical questions provide an important and necessary diversion from the task of working through thoughts and feelings. At other times, these practical questions are of more importance than the emotional or thinking concerns of the worrying person. The helper needs to ensure both that these practical questions are thought of and that the practical questions are used to help the work of worry not to divert the person from this work.

Worry work associated with loss, especially a forthcoming death, often induces a degree of depression. The person is depressed both by the implications the loss will have for the loser and for himself. The depression may take the form of interrupted sleep, changes in eating habits, lethargy and feelings of helplessness. These are natural responses to a significant loss. After all, the death of a person with whom one has lived and slept with or the death of a child are events to be depressed about. But the depression can become a form of loss in itself. Depressed worriers or losers can lose some of the features of the situation which are productive for them – the development of coping skills, the reworking of their traditional patterns of living and the development of new emotional strengths. The helper's task is both to accept that the depression sometimes experienced in anticipating a loss has a place in worry work, and to help the person engaged in this work to move beyond the depression. Some of the cognitive materials exercises provided later in this book (see pages 143 to 151) may be helpful for this purpose.

Conclusion

In this chapter we have explored the nature of loss, grieving and worry work and suggested some roles for helpers. In particular, we have given prominence to the idea that active worry work and grief work are essential if the loss is to be coped with and if the loss is to have meaning for the persons affected. Loss is not an easy subject to write about or to share with others. Yet some losses are inevitable. It is important to recognize that the community in which we live sometimes makes loss difficult to cope with. Grief work and worry work do, however, enable the person to come to terms with his loss and the reactions of others.

CHAPTER 10

RAPE

Introduction

In the first chapter of this book we made a distinction between various types of crisis events. In particular, we described some events which were not anticipated and which were external to the person. Rape is one of these events. We have chosen to examine rape as a crisis experience for a number of reasons. First, it is a genuine and deeply felt crisis experience for almost all who experience it. Few can come through the trauma of a violent sexual assault without experiencing a crisis of some kind. Second, unlike many other situations we have examined, rape is experienced predominantly by women. Though instances of homosexual rape are increasing slightly, the crime of rape is increasing steadily. Finally, many men who have written about rape have studied the psychology of the attacker. Our concerns here are with the effects of the attack and the experience of rape upon the victim.

Before looking at the reactions, thoughts and feelings of the victims of rape, some comments about their assailants may help to clarify why experiences of rape can be very different from victim to victim.

The Rapist

A common image of rape involves a stranger leaping out of a dark alleyway or side-street and attacking a woman he has never seen before. The common image also presupposes that the rapist is mentally 'sick' in some way and that the expression of his sickness is his attack upon the innocent woman. Yet one-third of all rapes take place in the home of the victim and are committed by someone known to the victim. As one rape crisis worker observed, 'It is very common for a woman to be raped by a man who has taken her out to dinner . . . he expects sex in return . . . an increasing number of girls working in offices have to suffer pressure to have sex – sex against your will in order to keep your job counts as rape. . . . Some girls are forced to have sex at college or university in exchange for the promise of good grades. . . . Some wives are raped by their husbands.' Rape is therefore possible under a variety of circumstances, not all of which involve strangers. Indeed, rape has been seen by some as a symbol of the sexual repression of women by men.

Given these very different circumstances for rape it is not easy to offer any meaningful understanding of the motives of the rapist. Paul Bowden, a psychologist at the Maudsley Hospital in London, has suggested that there are, however, a number of clearly identifiable types of rapists. First there is the rapist who is 'explosive'. He works through a rape fantasy in his mind several times and then seeks to turn his fantasy into reality by picking a girl who fits the image of his fantasy victim. Often this type of assailant is shy and sexually naîve, having some sexual desires which he regards as 'deviant' and which make him feel guilty about wanting sex. The second type identified by Bowden is a latent homosexual who commits rape in order to demonstrate to himself that he is not homosexual – that is is possible for him to desire and achieve sexual satisfaction with a woman. The third type of rapist in Bowden's classification is an 'aggressive sadistic' type who harbours a deep-seated and permanent hatred of women. He displaces his hatred of particular women (e.g., mother, sister, girlfriend) by attacking strangers. A fourth type is the 'sex-aggressive-diffusion' assailant who is sexually impotent unless a woman resists – he can only maintain his sexual excitement by being aggressive towards women. The final type is the 'aggressive anti-social criminal' who commits rape because he obtains pleasure from doing wrong, no matter what the wrongdoing. All of these types describe the rapist who is a stranger, though some descriptions will also apply to a rapist known to the victim. The one thing all have in common is that they use sex and aggression to humiliate and abuse women.

One other piece of information about rapists needs to be borne in mind throughout this chapter. It is that few rapists are ever regarded by the courts as being mentally ill. In 1975 fewer than 2.5% of those convicted of rape were sent for psychiatric treatment – this figure is no higher than the national average for mental illness. Rape is not regarded by legal minds as a reflection of a sexual or mental 'sickness'. What this suggests is that the sexual exploitation of women and violence against women is viewed strangely by our legal process. For those who have been raped would rarely suggest that their attackers were mentally 'normal'.

The Act of Rape

The three cases of rape we describe here illustrate clearly the humiliating experience that rape can be. We present these cases for two reasons. First, they provide dramatic illustrations of the severity of rape as a traumatic experience, and second, they provide materials which illustrate that rape is a very different experience for different women. These accounts are provided by three victims of rape and are detailed descriptions of the actual events. Whilst some may find these descriptions shocking, they are by no means untypical of the estimated 4750 rapes committed in England and Wales in the last year. The case of Wendy, for example, shows clearly the brutality of rape and the callousness of the attacker. It is important for those who wish to help the victim of rape that they understand both what has happened to the person, what reactions this has given rise to for the victim and how they as a helper react to what has happened to the victim. The brutality of the descriptions here (verbatim accounts from victims we have counselled) make it clear that the helper has first to overcome their own reactions to the rape before they can help the victim.

Wendy is a twenty-year-old office worker who enjoys dancing and music. She frequently goes to discotheques with her friends and has had a succession of boyfriends since she was sixteen. Usually she takes careful steps to ensure her safety on returning from her evenings out, but on this occasion she decided to walk home from a dance – a distance of less than a kilometer. Her own words describe the events after leaving the club:

'The first I knew was when this man stopped and asked me for a light for his cigarette. I was looking in my handbag and he suddenly walked behind me and grabbed my throat. He said "one scream and I'll slit your throat". I saw he had a big knife. I could feel myself going weak. I could hear my mother's voice saying "always come home with two or three others". I was immediately terrified of what they would think if I was raped, but I still wasn't sure what was going to happen to me.

'He hissed at me and spat at me, told me to do exactly as he said or else he would cut my face and cut one of my nipples off. I started to sob and to tremble. I really thought he would and that whatever I did he would do it. The worst part of this was that I could see in my mind what he would do and what it would mean for me. You know how they say that, as you're dying your whole life goes in front of you, well, as he was saying these things to me my whole future life flashed in front of me. It was awful . . . so humiliating and so frightening.

'He dragged me to an old disused building and we went inside. He was still holding me by the throat and I was beginning to choke and feel sick. He hissed at me again and bit my ear very hard. He said this was just to show that he meant to hurt me if I didn't do as he had asked. The room we were in was very small, there was no way I could get out without him grabbing me and, anyway, I was too frightened. I said that I would do anything he asked me to do, as long as he didn't cut me. He just laughed and said he might cut me, unless I was very good.

'He told me to get undressed. I started to take my clothes off. He was still holding on to me. He wanted me to talk to him about my body – to use dirty words to describe it to him. I said that I would, but didn't really know what he wanted me to say. He wanted to hear me talk about my "tits" and my "cunt" and about "fucking", so I did. It was awful. I hate to hear these words and here I was having to speak them. After a while I was naked and trembling. He told me to kneel in front of him and to take his thing in my mouth. I did. I was nearly sick, but thought that if I was sick he might cut me. He told me to suck it like an ice-lolly. I did. After a few minutes he came in my mouth and told me to swallow it all. I did. It was terrible.

'For about an hour I had to do all sorts of things and he did all sorts of things to me. He had intercourse with me, he tied me up with a rope he had with him – an old clothes line it was – and he buggered me and stuck a Guiness bottle up me. When he'd finished he took all my clothes with him, except for my raincoat and my shoes. I had to go home in just my coat and shoes. My parents were in bed. I just went to bed and wept all night and was sick the next day. I told my mother about it and we went to the police.'

Wendy's experience of rape has many characteristics which are common to other cases. Her humiliation involved the use of objects to satisfy the assailant's demands and also involved her in performing more and more forms of sex as a part of her humiliation. The rape was associated with violence, both actual (the biting and the sexual acts themselves) and threatened. Wendy may have managed to avoid even more violence being committed by the co-operation she showed, since there is some evidence that resistance leads to more violence. Finally, her humiliation involved not just the rape itself but also her thoughts and feelings about the effects the rape would have upon her relationship with her parents and others. The assailant's stealing of her clothing was a final humiliation.

Jean is eighteen and a college student living in a flat near the college. One day she returned to the flat early in the afternoon. At about three pm she heard a knock at the door. As she opened it two men burst into the room. One grabbed her and held his hand over her mouth whilst the other started searching the room. They were looking for things to steal. Jean described the event as follows:

'The one who had grabbed me held on to me very tight. He kept saying "try anything funny and its curtains for you", but he didn't say what he would do. I was too frightened anyway to say anything. After about twenty minutes the other man had finished searching the room. He told his friend that he'd had a good look round and could only find £40. The one that was holding me took me to the bedroom and threw me on the bed. He said they'd rape me if I didn't tell them where all the money was. Even though I told them that I didn't have any more, he continued to insist that I'd be raped if I didn't tell him where the money was. I realized that they were going to rape me anyway and I just broke down and cried and sobbed.

'Both of them were in the room and they started pulling my clothes off. When I was naked they started pumelling me and feeling all over me. It was like having a thousand hands grabbing at your body – they weren't gentle in any way. They both had intercourse with me, one after the other. It was very painful. Then they both decided to masturbate me. I couldn't believe my own body, but I actually had an orgasm and this set them off again. At that moment and ever since I have hated my own sexual feelings. They both masturbated over me, coming in my face and hair. One of them then started to turn me over saying he wanted to "fuck her arse". I passed out at the thought of this and when I came round they were gone.

Jean's reaction to rape was more concerned with fear than with humiliation. She was afraid that she would find herself in the same situation on some future occasion. The feeling of continuing vulnerability rather than humiliation at being raped was dominant in all discussions with Jean.

Sarah's experience of rape is quite different from that reported by both Wendy and Jean. For Sarah was raped by one of her colleagues at work. Sarah is thirty-two and has been a third-grade typist for six years. Following some re-organization of the office in which she worked a vacancy had arisen for a fourth-grade and senior position. Sarah was more than anxious to secure this new post. One evening a partner in the company asked her to come into his office just before she was due to leave home. He started to talk about the possibility of promotion. He hinted that several people were being considered for the new position, but that Sarah's chances looked reasonable on paper. She said that she was anxious to achieve promotion. Sarah then describes what happened:

'After talking about the job for about forty minutes – everyone else had gone home – he asked me if I wanted a drink. He gave me a gin and tonic. After a few more drinks and a lot of talk, he came over to me and said that he could get me the job if I co-operated. I said I didn't know what he meant. He took gentle hold of me and gave me a kiss. I was a little startled at first, but thought that this was all he wanted, so I co-operated. He took my co-operation as a green light and started to undress me. When I resisted, he laughed and said that he'd never thought of me as one who liked to fight before they screwed. I was horrified. The next twenty-five minutes were hell. I struggled to get away, but he'd locked the room and eventually he had his way with me. I was sobbing and crying. As he was getting dressed he just said that I'd enjoyed it really, and that he would put a good word in for me when the promotion came up. With that he left the room and I was left to sort myself out as best I could.

'I went straight home and had a drink. I live on my own. After a night of agony, I decided not to report him to the police or say anything at work, but that I would just keep my distance. I decided that it was, in any case, in part my fault.

'Two weeks later I was promoted to the new position and was sickened by it. He had cheapened not only me but also the work I did. I left the company some two months later and have been out of work since. You'll never believe how miserable that man has made me.'

Sarah's case differs from those of Wendy and Jean in two important respects. First, her assailant was not only known to her, he was someone she continued to associate with. Second, one feature of her response to being raped was that it was in part her fault – something neither Wendy nor Jean thought of in relation to their own circumstances. A further difference concerns her decision to keep quiet about the fact that she had been raped. In Britain in 1979 (the last year for which figures are available) there were 1170 women who reported rape. Official estimates and informal estimates from those who work to help rape victims put the figure of raped women at three times or more the number of reported cases since so many women are afraid of admitting they have been raped or do not wish to go through the procedures involved with reporting a rape.

Reactions to Rape

The three cases noted in this chapter illustrate that reactions to rape amongst victims are similar in certain respects and different in others. For example, all felt humiliated and fearful and anxious. All cried and felt powerless against their attackers. But not all dealt with their feelings in the same way. Sarah, as we have just observed, kept her feelings to herself whilst both Wendy and Jean reported their rapes to the authorities (medical and police) and discussed their experiences with others.

There have been a number of studies of the patterns of response of rape victims to their experiences. The most detailed of these is provided by Sandra Sutherland and Donald Scherl, two Americans who work in community mental health centres. They suggest that response to rape follows a number of stages. These are: (a) acute reaction, (b) outward adjustment, and (c) integration and resolution. We shall describe each of these stages in detail below, but first there is a need to recognize some of the immediate reactions to rape reported by victims.

Some Physical Reactions

Whatever psychological reactions to rape the person experiences, there are also physical reactions to be considered. Here are some statements made by rape victims during the first forty-eight hours after their ordeals:

> My ribs are so sore – I can't rest or sleep on this side . . . the pain just stays there, it's not getting worse or better . . . it's going to be a permanent pain, I know it is . . .

> It hurts to swallow and to eat . . . sometimes, I find myself breathing funnily. The doctors have not found anything, even after the X-ray, but I feel that there is something physically wrong . . .

> I get so many headaches now . . . I never used to get them . . . I'm sure that he's done some damage to me . . . after all, he knocked me about a lot before he had his way with me. . . . It was a bit like fighting with Mohamed Ali . . . If you're only nine stone in weight, it must do some real damage.

In addition to these physical consequences of injury, many rape victims experience sleep disturbance and a disturbance of well-established eating patterns. There are also likely to be physical symptoms associated with those areas of their body which were the direct focus of the attack. Those victims forced to have oral sex often report irritations in the mouth and throat and develop a range of dental problems; those forced to have normal intercourse frequently report vaginal discharge, itching, a burning sensation on urination and searing pain when intercourse is first attempted by their normal sexual partner; those victims who have suffered the humiliation and indignity of being forced to have anal sex often complain of anal bleeding and develop symptoms most commonly associated with haemorroids. There is a tendency in much of the writing about rape to see these complaints as largely psychosomatic. Yet in a number of cases in which the psychosomatic tag has been attached to the physical complaints of the victim, the physical conditions have indeed been as reported. There is a danger, therefore, that the psychological reactions to rape become so dominant that other reactions are ignored or are subsumed. Given the fact that some of the physical consequences of rape can be serious, it is generally desirable for the victim to see a doctor (especially in relation to both the question of pregnancy and venereal disease) even if the police are not to be involved. Whilst the medical examination is thorough, it is sometimes experienced as humiliating. The presence of a friend or helper at the examination is usually both permitted and desirable.

Having established the nature and significance of the physical reactions to rape, it is necessary to examine the psychological reactions. It should be stressed that the model to be described below, based on our own work with rape victims and the work of many others (see especially Burgess and Holmstrom, 1979), begins with the fear reactions of victims rather than with feelings of humiliation. Rape victims in our experience fear their own pain, fear the recurrence of the incident, fear the reactions of others and fear the consequences for their personal and social lives. Humiliation plays a part in the sequence of reactions we describe here, but the essential element in the course of recovery from rape is fear.

Stage 1: Acute Reaction

In the first few hours and days after being raped, the woman concerned has many thoughts, feelings and physical reactions. Uppermost amongst these reactions are fear, shock, anger, disbelief and dismay. Some, like Sarah, feel a sense of guilt about their complicity in the rape. Others feel humiliated both by the experience itself and by the embarrassment associated with disclosing the fact of rape to others. Most are fearful and anxious about both themselves and the reactions of others.

Whilst these are initial reactions, shock and dismay are soon replaced by other emotions, most especially anxiety. The triggers to anxiety in this stage are thoughts about consequences. Amongst these thoughts the following figure prominently:

Should I tell my parents – if I do, what will be the consequences?

Should I press legal charges – if I do, will this mean that my actions will be questioned in court and how will this make me feel?

Will I be able to identify the rapist and how will I feel if I should see him again?

Will neighbours and friends find out about the rape – will they blame me for it?

Will I become pregnant and what should I do if I am?

Will I get a venereal disease and what will it mean if I do?

Will being raped affect my sex life and if so how?

Will my boyfriend react sympathetically to all this or will he reject me?

Will being raped affect my relationships with other men, at work perhaps?

These thoughts are held as long as the actions they are associated with have not been performed. Once parents or boyfriend have been told, the anxiety may change or be reduced, but will not disappear for some time. In part this is because others tend to be more supportive than the victim anticipates and in part because some of the anxiety they report, whilst attached to the specific questions listed above (and others), is in fact non-specific anxiety – they just generally feel anxious about their security and well-being.

It is important to recognize the non-specific nature of the fear and anxiety which many rape victims report at this stage. For much of this non-specific anxiety can be traced back to the cultural view of sex outside marriage and of the complicity of women in rape. In Christian and other cultures, sex outside of marriage is still thought to be sinful and remains a major cause of conflict between those who engage in extra- or pre-marital sex and those who believe in chastity before marriage and faithfulness within it. Some regard rape as a just punishment for girls and women who engage in sexual activities outside of marriage – it is a punishment for tempting sex or being engaged in sex. Others tend to regard the woman as more likely to be a willing partner in rape than a victim, given their view of a woman as the 'respondent' in a sexual situation rather than as a person with self-ownership of her body. It is surprising just how much cultural and social assumptions play a key part in the reactions of the victim during this stage of the rape-reaction process.

The behaviour of some in both medical establishments and the police can, however, prolong the period of acute reactions. As one rape crisis worker observed, 'The police can often be so insensitive to the feelings of the victim and so questioning of the reality of their claims or of their complicity in the rape that the woman feels it was easier to cope with the rape itself.' Some doctors have reported rape to the police against the express wishes of their patients, thus involving the patient in unnecessary anxiety and feelings of guilt. One reason for suggesting that the victim be accompanied by a person in whom they have confided when visiting the police or a doctor is to have an ally in case the doctor or police-person is unsupportive or unthinking in their actions. Often the victim is unable to look after her own best interests, but she is able to entrust some of her interests to her friend or helper.

During this stage, victims of rape can best be helped by:

Being encouraged to express their feelings and anxieties and to share their memories of the rape and their views of its consequences with others, provided that the persons they share their thoughts and feelings with accept them as people and recognize that these reactions are both normal and necessary;

Not being asked 'why' questions, such as why did you go there or why didn't you fight back or why didn't you scream – such questions sound accusatory and tend to encourage the victim to explore issues which are of secondary (if any) importance to her at this time;

Encouraging practical steps to be taken, especially in relation to the questions about pregnancy and venereal disease; these practical steps may also involve the victim being accompanied by another person when she tells her parents, friends or boyfriends about her experiences;

After a time, encouraging the victim to talk through the longer-term implications of the rape for marriage, dating, self-protection;

Ensuring that someone is available for her to talk to when she feels the need to talk to someone; and finally

Not pressing her to inform the police or parents or anyone until she is ready to do so.

Whilst the work of rape crisis centres follows a similar form to the scheme outlined here, not every area has such a centre and many friends become the 'front line' helpers in such situations. These brief notes are intended to provide a broad indication of a helping strategy. The key is to accept the victim and to encourage the open expression of her inner feelings, whilst helping her to take some practical steps to help herself.

Stage 2: Outward Adjustment

After a time, as she grows out of the acute stage and the anxiety associated with it, the victim returns gradually to work or to college or to school and 'picks up the pieces' of her everyday life. It seems to others, and sometimes to the victim, that she has adjusted again to the 'real world' and that she is over the immediate crisis of being raped.

Most often, this period of seeming adjustment is the beginning of a complex coping process, involving the victim in both *denial* and *suppression* – the personal impact of what has happened is sublimated in the interests of both self and others. Anne Burgess and Lynda Holmstrom of Boston in the USA describe this suppression in the following way:

> the person tries to put the memory of rape completely out of her mind through a conscious effort. Victims using this mechanism do not like the subject of rape to be brought up ('Don't refresh my mind to it') and talk in terms of being able to 'block the thoughts' from their minds or actively keeping the thoughts from entering their minds. Victims using this mechanism often have previous experience of using this mechanism ('it's better not to think of the rape so you don't get bummed out').
> (Recovery from Rape, *American Journal of Psychiatry*, 1979 (October) page 1280.)

Suppression is not the only coping device used at this stage. Minimization is another. Here, the victim seeks to minimize in her mind the severity of the event for her. One sixty-year-old victim who had been beaten during her rape and cut in the stomach by the assailant's knife simply told herself that 'It would have been worse if this had happened when I was twenty or if I was a virgin – but I know what sex is about.' Other minimization strategies involve comparing her own rape with other, more violent or complex rapes and thinking, 'Well, I didn't get the worst.' Alternatively, actual rapes are compared with a fantasy of rape and are found not to be as severe.

Helpers are sometimes tempted to challenge these kinds of thoughts and to confront the underlying emotions that the victim is seen to be hiding.

This does not seem to be an appropriate strategy and may in fact prolong recovery from rape. A more appropriate helping strategy is to be supportive of the victim, to be involved with the victim's relatives and friends so as to help them understand the feelings and thoughts she is experiencing and to minimize the negative effects of their comments and actions upon her (e.g., reminding her of the need to take a different route home; making comments about the reactions of others, and to anticipate the next stage of recovery.

Stage 3: Integration

The beginning of this phase is often triggered by some specific event. For example, the victim receives a summons to appear in court to give evidence against her assailant, or the victim sees someone resembling her attacker or she discovers that she is pregnant. The phase is characterized by obsessive thoughts about the rape and by feelings of depression and worthlessness.

Two issues need to be resolved during this stage. These are her feelings about her attacker and her feelings about herself. Helpers need to exercise considerable care in helping the victim examine these feelings about herself. For example, she is likely to express feelings of guilt about the attack – it was partly my fault'. If the helper is too eager to challenge this assumption, she may feel that she is not being understood. It is best to encourage her to talk through her feelings about herself without trying to resolve those feelings for her – let her do the work, prompt her to work.

There will be many issues she will have to work on. Not all will concern the rape itself. For the crisis experience of rape often forces the person to review her ways of thinking and feeling in general. A good many fears, phobias, negative feelings and other reactions are likely to come into the sphere of attention at this time. Included amongst them could be one or more of the following:

Feeling unsafe where she lives

A fear of men – or if not fear, having strong negative feelings towards men, including men she had previously thought highly of

A fear of sex – this is an especially strong feeling for those victims who, prior to the rape, had been virgins

Fear of venereal disease and pregnancy – even after a visit to a doctor and a firm indication that neither is going to happen, the victim can continue to fear that the doctor got it wrong and that she will, after all, have a baby or contract venereal disease

Feelings of anger or revenge – sometimes these feelings are out on the surface, but often anger is felt but repressed, only occasionally coming to the surface

Feeling depressed

Feeling guilty

Feeling shameful about the fact that it has happened at all

Feeling worthless – as if the rape has so belittled her that there is no worthwhile reason for continuing to function

Feeling irritable – with others, with self, with helpers and with anything

Feeling un-sexy

Having the same thoughts over and over again

Feeling misunderstood

With all of these feelings (and others) the helper's task is to encourage the person to disclose her feelings in a way that is comfortable to her (see the counselling techniques described in Chapter 11) whilst at the same time accepting these feelings and reacting genuinely to them without giving advice. Throughout, the aim is to help the victim to return to her pre-rape life-style as quickly as possible.

In looking at the feelings of the victim towards the assailant, the helping person needs to permit anger to be expressed unchecked for some time. Frequently this anger will be distorted and redirected towards herself, thereby feeding her feelings of guilt and depression, but it is essential that the anger she feels is worked through in some way. The aim throughout this stage is to help the victim both express her inner feelings and to enable her to seek a resolution of these feelings.

Clearly, resolving feelings about being raped is not easy and not all women are able to achieve a resolution easily or without help. It is worth remembering that there are certain signs that can be looked for which help to identify someone requiring more professionalized help at this stage. These signs include: (a) continued disruption of normal sleeping and eating habits; (b) the expression of generalized and new fears about a range of circumstances; or (c) engaging in obsessive rituals, especially those which seek to avoid contact with any male. Rape crisis centres will provide valuable assistance for the victims of rape at this and other stages.

Conclusion

Recovery from rape is not an easy achievement. In several studies the period of recovery has been shown to range from four to five months to ten years. The stage described briefly above may, therefore, take many years to complete. Not all victims will recover their self-respect. Some will take to drink or unnecessary medication as a way of coping with their feelings and a small number may try to commit suicide. But the majority of women, given time and a great deal of support, are able to come to terms and cope with the crisis resulting from rape.

PART THREE: COPING

11 Self-help and Coping

12 Mutual Aid, Help and Support

INTRODUCTION

The first part of this book was concerned with the concepts of crisis and coping. Our concern was to examine the ideas behind these concepts and to make them more accessible to others.

The second part of this book has been concerned with selected crisis experiences. We selected a number of experiences which permit the examination of the structure of crisis reactions and the nature of the helping strategies that may be employed by professionals, para-professionals, friends and family. Some of these chapters concerned normal development (e.g., adolescence, early adulthood, ageing) and others examined specific kinds of crisis experiences. These chapters were selective – they reflect our own interests in crisis experiences and helping. Many other chapters could have been included. The point to note, however, is that the structural basis of the crisis experiences we have described is often present in other crisis experiences. In particular, the model of loss (see Chapter 9) seems to us to be a valuable model with wide applicability.

This final section has one over-riding concern. This is to outline some specific ideas about helping. These are ideas about both the nature of helping (strategies) and specific ways of helping (tactics). We outline these strategies and tactics for helpers of all kinds – professionals and friends alike. We want to stress to those seeking to help others that they need to use the three basic conditions of helping: empathy, warmth and genuiness (see pages 00 to 00) on any occassion on which helping is attempted. They also need to be sensitive to the needs and responses of the person they seek to help. The tactics we describe are potentially helpful if used sensitively, carefully and confidently. They are also potentially unhelpful if used uncaringly, haphazardly, despairingly or without sensitivity to the reaction of the person being helped.

In a book of this size and scope, the descriptions of helping we provide here will necessarily be brief. This is not an encyclopedia of helping strategies and practices. It is selective. There are many other techniques and tactics available. The reader should regard these two chapters as starting points for the exploration of ways of helping.

CHAPTER 11

SELF-HELP AND COPING

Introduction

The previous section of this book was devoted to descriptions of specific forms of crisis. Three key themes are a consistent feature of these earlier chapters. First, coping and crisis cannot be regarded as simply questions of the psychological well-being of the affected person. The coping strategy a person adopts will need also to deal with that person's social position and the impact of the community upon them. That is to say, all of the crisis events we have described have a clear social element which helpers need to be aware of when developing coping skills. Second, particular crisis-laden situations – divorce, unemployment and job-loss, rape, ageing – are experienced differently by each individual. Whilst we have provided a framework for understanding some features of these particular crises, our frameworks may only be appropriate for some. It is more important to understand the motives, thoughts, feelings and actions of the person in crisis than to try and fit him into the particular frameworks we have documented here. Further, we have suggested that some events which many regard as crisis situations – unemployment being a good example – are not experienced as crisis events by some people but are rather felt to be points of development. Crisis thus holds the possibility for transition learning and personal development. This leads to the third consistent message of the last eight chapters. Crises are a normal feature of development. The attempt to help a person through a crisis and the related attempt to develop and enhance coping skills are aimed more at ensuring that the learning potential of a crisis is maximized and the distress implicit in the crisis is minimized. The chapters dealing with adolescence, mid-life and growing older reflect the development nature of crises – they are not all situational.

The first two chapters of this book sought to examine both the nature of crisis and the nature of coping. These last two chapters seek to bring together the preceding ten chapters by documenting specific actions which individuals and others can take to help a person in crisis and to show how these actions relate back both to the specific crisis situations we have described and to the models of crisis and coping we have outlined.

Before documenting some specific coping tactics, it is important to stress a number of points.

First, helping a person in crisis is not a task reserved for professionals. Whilst the services of doctors, counsellors, social workers, marriage guidance cousellors, rape crisis centre workers and others may be regarded as necessary for the person, the help afforded by relatives, friends and work-mates is often as important if not more important. When a person is divorcing, friends often carry the burden of sharing and helping. When a person is bereaved, friends and workmates are often the only persons from whom help is sought. Whilst we do not deny the place of the professional in certain helping situations, we are primarily concerned with the possibilities for helpers – no matter who they are. Helping is a feature of the community, not an exclusive right conferred by training.

Second, whilst there are several sets of skills which helpers can develop, helping as a process depends on a small number of basic conditions. These are: (a) empathy – the ability to share another person's thoughts and feelings as if they were one's own without ever loosing that 'as if' quality; (b) warmth – respecting and accepting the person for what they are, not for what they used to be or might become and showing this respect through an open and caring relationship; (c) genuineness – the helper is reacting not simply as a person who is there to help a person out of a crisis, but as a person who is sharing that crisis at that time with that person; (d) minimum vulnerability – the helper has to avoid becoming a part of the person's problem and has to work at becoming a part of the solution to their problem. In short, these conditions say that the person seeking to help a person in crisis needs to be involved not simply as a helper but as a whole person. A helper is making a commitment to genuine psychological and personal contact with the person in crisis.

Third, a person in crisis sometimes needs to be advised. They need to be encouraged to think about reporting a rape to the police or to a doctor; they need to be encouraged and advised to examine their rights to benefit if they lose their job; they need to be advised to consider the social and personal implications of divorce. But advice is just that; it is not a set of directives. If a person rejects advice that is their right, and the respect a helper should have for these rights should be total. If a person rejects the advice of a helper he is not rejecting the helper, he is acting with the knowledge of the advice given. But most of the situations we have described require more than advice-giving. They require a concerted attempt to understand the situation the person is in and the motives that led to that situation; they require the helper to understand and know of the thoughts, feelings and actions the person engages in; the helper needs to be aware of the attempts that the person has made to cope and the reasons for the success and failure of these attempts; they often require the person to share their pain or hurt or anxiety or distress. Whilst advice-giving has a place in the process of helping, it is but a part of the helping task.

Fourth, the helper's task is not always to make the situation the person is experiencing less distressing, though this clearly is the ultimate goal. Sometimes, the helper needs to confront the person in crisis so as to achieve a significant development in his or her attempts to cope. Confrontation is not an easy task for a helper. It has to be completed in a situation in which the person in need trusts and accepts the helper and also knows that the confrontation will not lead to rejection by the helper if the right answers are not produced. Confrontation works best when conducted in an atmosphere of empathy, warmth, genuineness and mutual respect.

Finally, in many situations helpers do not know the answers. Indeed, for many situations there are no answers. Helpers can never say with any conviction, 'if I were you', because each person's crisis is unique. What a helper is able to do is to help the person in crisis explore the possible answers that might apply to them. But this is no easy task. It is made more difficult if the helper is seeking to make judgements about the person is trying to help. Effective helping depends upon mutuality; mutuality is often broken by one person judging another in such a way as to belittle or deny some feature of that person.

In describing particular helping tactics, therefore, it is assumed that the helper is aware of the assumptions outlined here. For the points made so far in this chapter act as a backcloth to the tactics described in the final section of this book.

Self-help

The next chapter deals with helping through such diverse activities as massage (for the reduction of physical stress), the development of social support organizations and co-counselling. It takes as its theme the idea that some helping activities require another person or group of people to be present at a particular time if the form of coping they wish to use is to be effective. It develops the idea that a person in crisis can be enabled to help themselves more directly. We will describe here a number of coping tactics which can be used to help a person cope with the physical stress to which crises can give rise; with the thoughts that a person in crisis has and with the feelings that accompany the experience of crisis. Whilst another person may be needed to initiate the affected person into these particular coping tactics, they are all essentially forms of self-help.

Self-help and the Body

Earlier in this book (see Chapter 2, pages 28–29) we documented a form of relaxation training and suggested that the technique was important in the context of helping to reduce body tension. The particular tactic described is a short form of a complex relaxation system. More elaborate styles of relaxation exist and are well documented in books about yoga or in texts dealing with what is known as systematic relaxation (see for example, Carkhuff, 1969).

Relaxation is one way of reducing stress in the body. Another way is activity. Jogging, shouting, squash-playing – any short and intensive way of releasing energy from within the body – getting the energy converted into action – can be useful in reducing tension or arousal. People who are in stressful conditions (whatever the cause) can find high-energy activity useful. Though there is a need for care – jogging and sport can be a danger to health unless they are gradually developed by the person – these kinds of activity are a useful adjunct to other forms of self-help.

The causes of some stresses are physical. For example, there is good evidence that diet is associated with migraine – a concentration on cheese and chocolate coupled with stress can produce migraine effects. Some of the physical effects of ageing are due more to diet than to age itself. Body maintenance is therefore an important tool in self-help. When a person is in crisis diet, sleep and exercise often suffer. It is important that, once the more immediate needs of the person in crisis are being attended to, the bodily needs of the person are attended to. The *Good Health Guide* (Open University, 1979) is a sourcebook for activities and information which can be useful in dealing with the physical needs of the person in crisis.

Thoughts, Feelings, Actions and Self-help

A number of crisis events occur because of the way in which people think about themselves in relation to others. Albert Ellis, an American psychotherapist, has suggested that irrational thoughts are at the root of many personal difficulties which develop into crises. He has developed a system of helping that is based on the attempt to identify the irrational beliefs a person holds. In order to help the person it is necessary to change these beliefs so that they are more rational, so that they take fuller account of the reality of the situation in which the person actually finds himself so that he is better able to cope. His basic proposition is that thoughts determine the way we act and feel in relation to crisis events (Ellis, 1962).

Ellis defines an irrational belief in terms of three conditions: (1) the beliefs cannot be proven or disproven – others involved in the same situation have very different beliefs which are equally valid; (2) the beliefs lead to unpleasant feelings (e.g., anxiety; which are unnecessary, given the situation in which the person finds himself; and (c) they prevent the person from going back to the situation in which he finds himself and looking at it more objectively and finding ways of resolving his distress. Whilst there are many irrational beliefs, Ellis identifies eleven which he says are ubiquitous in Western civilization (Ellis, 1962, p.61). We present these below together with occasional examples and explanations. In reading this list, it is important that the self-help value of such a list is realized. For if persons in crisis can be helped to understand that a part of their crisis may relate to their beliefs then they begin to be in a position to work on changing their own irrational assumptions. Helpers might usefully engage the person in the task of identifying the extent to which this list or a part of it can help the person account for his or her crisis.

1 It is absolutely essential for an individual to be loved by every person in their environment.

   Mike had worked hard to gain promotion but was surprised at the speed at which he moved into middle management. Each time he made a decision, though, few actually approved of it. Soon, going to work became a crisis event – each day could only be faced after some alcohol. Within five months of promotion, Mike was a confirmed alcoholic and was eventually dismissed from his job. He said to his helper at a sanitorium for alcoholics that 'nobody loves me. . . . I just wanted them to like me, and they hated me . . . drink was a way out of their hate.'

Whilst it is desirable for a person to be loved and liked by others, the idea that all should love and like a person is irrational because it is impossible to achieve. Striving to attain acceptance and love by everyone leads a person to lose self-control – their actions are motivated by their desire to please a person rather than the desire to maximize the benefits of a particular situation. In Mike's case, his desire to please everyone so that he could be liked in return lead to unwise management decisions and rejection of him by some of his staff and some of his superiors. His attempts to win back their acceptance led him to displease others. His actions became dominated by his desire to please others. In the end, he could not face himself. He was not self-directing.

Mike's therapy consisted of a confrontation between his actions and his beliefs. Over a period of months he began to recognize that respect at work is more related to demonstrable self-direction and real work achievement. Mike is once again trying to build up his career.

2 It is necessary for each individual to be completely competent, adequate and achieving in all areas if that individual is to be worthwhile.

Sarah is a medical student in her final year. She was referred to a counsellor following a series of fainting episodes and a number of crying fits which seemed to occur spontaneously. Sarah soon began to talk about her forthcoming final examinations. Her anxiety seemed to relate to the fact that on some papers she felt competent but on others she was sure that she was not going to do very well. Her tutors are convinced that she will pass her examinations without difficulty; she herself thinks that she will pass, but only just in some subjects. At the root of her difficulty seems to be the idea that nothing less than identical perform- ances – consistency – will be regarded as satisfactory. This belief, which is not an accurate reflection of either the examination system or the reality for most qualifying doctors, has become so dominant that it is disabling her revision and causing substantial anxiety.

The belief that Sarah has is irrational because so few are competent in all areas of medicine, because the examination system is not geared to measuring consistency in the way she imagined, because failure on some papers does not mean that she will not qualify. It is harmful as a belief because it leads her to fear failure more than she ought to and encourages anxiety. It is stressful because it leads her to feel that she is in competition with an idealized standard which she cannot attain. The distress she feels expresses itself physically in her fainting and crying and emotionally in her obvious distress. She was helped considerably by having this belief confronted and by being encouraged to take a more rational look at the nature of the examination system she was participating in. She is now a doctor in general practice.

3 If a person makes a mistake, then they are bad and should be punished.

After an office party, Jack made love to his secretary. Both regretted their love-making, since both were happily married and felt that their love-making had created a barrier between them which affected their working lives. Jack felt guilty. He felt that he should not have allowed himself to be carried away after the party and that he had shamed his wife and his secretary. He blamed himself and felt that he should be punished. He did not tell his wife about the party because he felt she would leave him, but his dishonesty towards her made him feel also that he should be punished. He tried to take an overdose.

Jack's suicide attempt surprised everyone – it seemed all out of proportion to the incident which triggered it. But his belief that he was guilty and should be punished had led him to this drastic action. When it failed and his wife was accepting of him, he still felt guilty about not telling her sooner – about the deceit. Jack needed to be encouraged to see that mistakes are not necessarily a reflection of badness – one mistake does not make a villain. His wife understood what had happened and how it had come about, and was accepting of him; she also understood that his motives did not represent any change in character. Jack himself had defined his love-play with his secretary as a mistake which deserved punishment. When Jack redefined the situation and was shown a high degree of acceptance by his wife, he was better able to cope.

4 It is terrible and catastrophic when things are not the way an individual wants them to be.

When Phil and Mary married. Mary expected Phil to be a loving husband and spend each of his evenings after work and all of his weekends with her. She expected him to have an interest in their house and to share all the interests in home affairs that she had. When he continued to go out two nights each week with his friends without her and went away to rugby matches most weekends in the rugby season, she concluded that he did not really love her. She left him after two years and returned to her family home. After three weeks, she agreed to see a marriage guidance counsellor.

The counsellor quickly recognized that the failure of Phil to meet Mary's expectations of him was at the root of their difficulties and that Mary had never made her expectations of Phil clear. There had been no negotiations about the nature of their domestic life. It also became clear that Mary's reaction to the real situation was based on the idea that if their domestic life was not perfect (Mary's word) then it must be awful. Mary was helped to see how most situations in life are not perfect and that life often involves some compromise between needs, wants and possibilities. The opening out of this discussion enabled Phil and Mary to negotiate their domestic life and Mary to accept the irrationality of her striving for perfection.

5 Unhappiness is a function of events outside the control of the individual.

David was a compulsive news follower. He listened to each hourly newscast between 7am and 11pm and read newspapers and news magazines avidly. All of the news he read made David unhappy. He felt that high levels of unemployment, wars in various parts of the world, continuing tension between the super-powers and the related arms race, the increase in levels of street violence, the industrial unrest in parts of the Western world, the plight of the Third World and many more issues were all tied to his inability to secure social change or political action. He wrote to newspapers regularly offering solutions to world problems, but his letters were never published. He occassionally stood in the streets and made speeches, but no one listened. He felt that the news was being ignored by many and that his solutions were rejected. He went on hunger strike for peace, but gave up after eleven days since no one had published his fast. When he talked about burning himself outside Parliament in the way that Buddhist monks did in Vietnam his relatives decided to seek the help of a psychiatrist.

David believed that his own unhappiness – and he was bitterly unhappy – was due entirely to events beyond his control. He did not see, until he was helped to see, that it was his perception of these events which caused him distress.

David's case is particularly dramatic, but is indicative of the way in which this particular irrational belief can affect a person. As Ellis observes, the last part of the statement sticks and stones may break my bones, but names will never hurt me is rarely believed.

6 If something may be dangerous, harmful or distressing then it is important to think about it constantly.

Albert had to have his leg amputated. He thought about the operation all the time and about the consequences it would have for him, but rarely shared his thoughts with others. He had concluded that the operation would be awful, that he would not be able to cope with the strain of being one-legged afterwards and that he would never be adequately rehabilitated back into his normal world. His stress on arrival at hospital was such that his blood pressure was dangerously high, and the operation had to be postponed on a number of occassions simply because he was too stressed.

Thinking constantly about situations does not change them. Thinking constantly about potential difficulties sometimes ensures that those difficulties will arise. Thinking about something constantly can actually make a situation worse than it actually is, as Albert's case shows. The rational person, according to Ellis, will review the situation objectively (almost as though it was happening to someone else) and develop some kind of strategy for dealing with its fearful elements. Whilst this does involve careful thought, it is not obsessive and not focused upon the problem but on development. Ellis suggests that such thought work is productive, but generalized worry work is counterproductive. This comes back to points made earlier: that it is the work of worry rather than the worry itself which can lead to more effective coping.

7 It is easier to run away from difficulties than it is to face them.

Whenever Jack and Angela's marriage became difficult one or other of them would go away for a few days in the hope that their difficulty would sort itself out. No matter how severe or trivial the difficulty, this was the solution they always pursued. After two and a half years they divorced. Jack said, 'We never really came to terms with being married.' After two years of separation, Jack and Angela re-married. They have been married now for eleven and a half years; whenever a difficutly arises they share it and examine ways of working through the difficulty.

During their first marriage, Jack and Angela discovered that whenever they waited for a difficulty to sort itself out the difficulty was always there on their return. What is more, they found that unresolved difficulties were cumulative – each new difficulty was added on to a catalogue of previous difficulties. A more rational approach to their difficulties has led Angela and Jack to have a much more successful second marriage.

8 Individuals need a stronger person than themselves to lean on.

When Mike's mother died he was twenty-three years old. He had always been at home. His mother had made his meals, bought his clothes, found his job for him, helped him with his night-school classes, managed his money for him, arranged his holidays . . . in fact she had done everything for him. Her sudden and unexpected death left him helpless as well as bereaved. His health deteriorated since he rarely cooked a meal; his appearance deteriorated as he hardly ever replaced ageing clothes; his financial affairs became chaotic since he had no skills in money management. He became ill and needed long periods away from work. He became depressed.

Mike's helpers – mainly friends – recognized that his dependence upon his mother now left Mike insecure and unskilled. He had never learnt to be self-directing and had few skills appropriate to self-care and development. They began to teach him skills and to decrease the dependence he had on others.

Mike is one example of dependency – there are many others. The common feature of these examples is the lack of self-direction they give rise to. This can be a major source of crisis not only when the prop on which the person has been dependent goes but also when the need for self-direction begins to be felt, but the person feels their entrapment in a dependent relationship.

9 Past events in an individual's life determine present behaviour and cannot be changed.

Sue had dated many men, but her relationships never lasted more than ten to eleven months. She now found it difficult to get beyond this time-span, even when she was with men she actually liked and felt she would wish to build relationships with. She said to her friend and counsellor, 'When it gets to ten months I just know it's all going to end . . . and soon after I begin to think that it does. . . . It's always been the same and always will be.' This is a source of distress for Sue, since she believes that because she can never make any kind of meaningful relationship with a man she must therefore be latently lesbian. This thought is causing her considerable distress because she does not think and feel like a lesbian, but says that she must be, because of her past record of relationships with men.

Sue needed to be helped to see that, whilst past events influence the present, they do not necessarily determine it. A person does have the capacity to learn from the past (as a number of cases throughout this book show) and is able to affect the present. It was Sue's belief that she was a passive captive of her history that gave rise to her distress.

10 An individual should be concerned and upset by the problems of other people.

This is irrational for two reasons. First, not all difficulties will affect us in the same way. Whilst we might feel and show concern for the distress experienced by someone close to us, we may not feel the same about the distress felt by someone with whom we are casually associated. Indeed, the distress some share with us may have no effect upon us at all. The second reason for regarding this belief as irrational is that becoming upset at the problems of others often makes it more difficult to be helpful towards them.

11 There is always a correct answer to any problem and it is catastrophic if it is not found.

There is no perfect solution to any of the situations we have described in this book. There are solutions which are appropriate at that time, but they generally represent less than the ideal for the person most affected. The search for perfect solutions, just like the search for a perfect relationship or job, is likely to produce frustration, anger and anxiety. It is also likely to produce permanent dissatisfaction on the part of the person who is searching, since they are constantly looking for a lost solution. Helpers need to take care that the resolution of a crisis is understood to involve resolution and disappointment. The person in crisis must not be led to believe that the resolution they achieve is without its own difficulties.

Few persons in crisis will recognize all of these eleven beliefs as applying to them. But many may recognize one or more of them. They need to be enabled to confront them, to understand the irrationality of the belief and to see ways in which change can lead to more effective coping.

There are some self-help methods that a person can use to help identify and change irrational beliefs and assumptions. The following four are especially useful:

1 Literal Description: write or taperecord a description of the situation in which the person finds himself and develop his understanding of the thoughts, feeling and actions which he is currently engaged in. It is important that this attempt to descibe is made as literal as possible, for the aim is to inject some objectivity into self-evaluation. The person needs to be encouraged to act as a witness to his situation.

2 Repetition: when engaged in thinking about his situation the person needs to be encouraged to identify key phrases or sentences which summarize for him some feature of the situation. These phrases, if repeated over and over again so that their full meaning is explored (try putting emphasis in different parts of the phrase), often lead to the meaning of the situation itself being clarified.

3 Association: encourage the person to understand his thoughts and feelings and then enable him to work back through his past so as to identify previous situations in which the same thoughts and feelings occurred. Encourage him to explore the relationship between these past occasions and the present so that he can begin to understand their meaning. Whilst there is a danger of encouraging him to believe that the present situation is simply a function of all previous situations (see irrational belief number 9 above), making connections and addressing the question 'what can I do to cope' can make this a constructive self-help activity.

4 Monodrama: many situations we have descibed in this book involve a number of other people. Monodrama seeks to aid the person more fully understand the motives, thoughts and feelings which others bring to the situation. Using different chairs to represent other persons, the affected person is asked to hold a discussion between himself and the others, with the affected person playing the parts of all the characters. This often produces insights and greater understanding. It is especially effective if the person is assisted by another person who knows of the situation, but is not directly involved.

These four specific techniques are helpful in encouraging persons to understand more of how their own perception and beliefs affect their current situations and the nature of their crisis. Though developed for co-

counselling purposes, it is possible for people in crisis to use these techniques in order to confront themselves and their beliefs. It is clearly helpful if they are assisted in this process at the beginning.

Dealing with irrational beliefs is one way of tackling the counterproductive thoughts that many experience whilst in crisis. Another important set of coping tactics is known as cognitive restructuring (Meichenbaum, 1977). Essentially, this is a series of activities designed to change the thoughts a person has. Whilst they may need help initially to achieve these changes, they generally develop the skill to use restructuring as a self-help tool.

There are two primary tasks when restructuring. The first is to relate the thought to here and now rather than past or future. Here and now is a term used in many texts about helping. It means right now, rather than any other time – it means focusing upon the present. A thought like 'I can never do anything that's any good' is a statement which does not relate to time. To make it a here and now statement, it is necessary to inject time statements into the thought. For example, this thought might become, 'Sometimes I feel that I can never do anything right; at other times, when things are fine, I don't think about my abilities; right now I feel vulnerable.' By injecting time into the thought and focusing upon the here and now, the thought becomes a more accurate balance sheet for the person. This highlights the second task in restructuring. The person needs to inject a sense of balance into the thought by checking his feelings of weakness against his feelings of strength. Thoughts that are restructured enable coping if they seek to identify both strengths and weaknesses. An example of this might be the restructuring of this thought:

I don't think anyone cares about me

into this thought:

When I was a child I had the sense that everyone was caring for me; now that I am older, I seem to be more alone; sometimes I like being alone, but right now I feel as if being alone means that no one cares about me.

The essential purpose of restructuring thoughts is to provide a basis for accurate understanding of the thoughts that determine action. It is a productive activity for a person seeking to enhance his coping skills.

Another productive activity concerns 'self-contracting'. Though it sounds complex, it is in fact relatively simple. The basic idea here is that it is helpful for a person in crisis to specify to himself a contract for change. Essentially, the person makes a contract with himself to change his thoughts or behaviour whenever the thoughts are 'negative' or he engages in behaviour which he is seeking to change. Dustin and George, two counsellors working in the USA (Dustin and George, 1973), suggest that the following six elements are necessary for an effective self-contract:

1 Clear expectations – the person needs to be clear about the behaviours or thoughts which he expects to be able to change;

2 Specificity – the person needs to clearly establish how much of a certain behaviour or what kind of thought will 'count' and what the rewards for changing the behaviour or thought will be; this generally means that the person needs to write down his contract, but it is necessary that he is specific about targets and rewards;

3 Monitoring – it is essential that the person records his behaviour and thoughts and his success at change and that he develops an honesty in monitoring himself. Those who have been on a diet will know how difficult this can be, but careful monitoring provides a clue to the extent of constructive self-help;

4 Sanctions – the person needs to establish whether his self-contract will involve sanctions – what happens if he continues to engage in behaviours or have thoughts which he is seeking to change?;

5 Reachable goals – it is essential that the person sets realistic targets for himself – unrealistic targets encourage frustration and anxiety;

6 Bonus systems – each self-contract can contain a bonus system that rewards adherence to the contract.

Whilst such a contracting regime may not appeal to all, it can be effective for some. A person may need to be helped in establishing a contract for himself, but many will be able to monitor their own progress.

The final set of tactics we include here is known under the general heading of assertiveness. Before describing some specific assertiveness tactics, it is necessary to clarify some assumptions about the nature of assertiveness and to distinguish between assertiveness and aggression. Aggression is usually some kind of expression which is inappropriate and achieved at the expense of others; assertiveness involves emotional honesty and self-expression whilst respecting the position of others. Aggression is characterized by righteousness and superiority, whereas assertiveness is characterized by confidence and self-respect. People value and respect assertiveness whilst they feel hurt and sometimes humiliated in the face of aggression. Whilst there is sometimes a fine line between aggression and assertiveness, there is such a thing as responsible assertiveness which can be productive for the person who practises it and can lead to the resolution of conflict and to more effective coping with stress.

Assertiveness is based upon a number of assumptions. These are summarized below:

1 We all have the right to respect from other people.

2 We all have the right to have needs and to have these needs recognized alongside the needs of others. We also have the right to ask that others respond to our needs and to decide whether we respond to theirs – we are not able to demand responses.

3 We have the right to have feelings and to express these feelings in ways which do not violate the dignity of other people (e.g., the right to feel sad, tired, happy, depressed, angry, sexy, lively).

4 We have the right to decide whether we will meet expectations others have of us. We have the right to change our minds. We need to exercise these rights in such a way as not to violate the rights of others.

5 We have the right to our own opinions and the right to express these opinions.

These rights, derived from Arthur Lange's and Patricia Jakubowski's accounts of assertiveness (Lange and Jakubowski, 1976), outline some of the important assumptions of assertiveness. They are also a statement of why many individuals find life stressful and crisis-laden. They feel either that they do not have these rights or that they are prevented from exercising them. The following tactics may be useful in developing assertiveness as a coping skill:

1 Reflection: rather than simply accepting statements from others, reflect them back by repeating the message of the statement in words with which the speaker feels comfortable;

2 Repeated assertion: if a point made is not heard or acknowledged, repeat the point until it is, whilst continuing to respond to points made by the other person;

3 Broken record: continue to repeat the message you wish to assert in the same form and in the same level tone until some action is taken;

4 Pointing out the implicit assumptions: by focusing upon what others are

taking for granted, it is possible for a person to assert his own interpretation of the situation in which he finds himself;

5 Questioning: this can sometimes be a useful method of assertion, especially if the questions are accepting of the rights of others as outlined above;

6 Paradoxical statements: here's a brief description of an incident that makes clear what a paradoxical statement is. A man wearing sun-glasses prescribed for him by a doctor is waiting for a train; an older man walks up to him and says, 'What's matter with you then, got a dud eye?' to which the first man replies, 'Now wouldn't you feel bad if I told you that I had!' The paradox comes from showing another person what their aggression might look like.

7 Fogging: when faced with a criticism, the person 'fogs' by accepting that there is probably some degree of truth implicit in the criticism, but is cautious about accepting its full force.

There are several texts in which these tactics are described in more detail. Two in particular are recommended for those wishing to develop such skills. They are:

Alberti, R. E. and Emmons, M.L (1974): *Your Perfect Right – A Guide to Assertive Behaviour*. USA: Impact Press.

Osborn, S. M. and Harris, G. G. (1975): *Assertive Training for Women*. Springfield, Ill.: Charles Thomas.

Like many of the techniques described in this chapter, the descriptions we provide here are brief and will need follow-up. But the point to note about these several techniques (irrational beliefs, cognitive restructuring, assertiveness training and self-contracting) is that they are tactics which the person can acquire for use in self-help so as to better cope with crises.

Conclusion

This chapter has been concerned to document some methods of self-help which the person in crisis can develop both to deal with his immediate situation and to use as coping tactics in his coping repertoire. This set of tactics is essentially psychological, dealing with the person as an individual. The chapter which follows offers materials and coping tactics dealing with mutual aid and help. In both these chapters it is assumed that a person can be helped towards developing a particular coping tactic by another and that the person is able to 'pick and mix' the way in which he uses these tactics. Helpers need to be eclectic in their work with a person in crisis. The materials in this chapter provide a beginning point for self-help which is itself eclectic.

CHAPTER 12

MUTUAL AID, HELP AND SUPPORT

Introduction

The previous chapter examined helping tactics which involve persons seeking to help themselves directly. Whilst some of the activities suggested there could benefit from the presence of an additional person (for example, the monodrama suggested could be enhanced by involving a second person as an observer and commentator), such involvement is not essential. In this chapter, the helping tactics presented require at least a second person to be involved. Indeed, some of the tactics developed here involve several others. Whilst these tactics look varied and diverse they do have one thing in common: they all involve the principle and practice of mutual aid for mutual benefit.

This chapter has benefited from the direct involvement of the authors in the work of the Mutual Support Network in Wales – a network which aims to help unemployed and unwaged persons respond to their own situation through their own efforts. The ideas behind and the achievements of that network have especially encouraged us to explore the basic principles of mutual aid, both at the level of the community and at the level of friendship groups and helping relationships.

The idea that a group of individuals or a community is a coping resource is not a new idea in this book. Throughout we have given emphasis to the idea that crisis situations have both a personal and a social component. For example, part of the difficulty in coping with divorce or bereavement relates to the way in which divorce and death are regarded in the community in which a person lives. Just as the community may make coping with divorce or death (or any of the crisis situations we have examined) more difficult, so too can the community be supportive and facilitative and enabling. A number of people working together to help one or more of its number cope with a crisis can not only help that person to cope but also enable others to improve their own ability to cope. They can change the milieu within which the person in crisis experiences that crisis and can help that person see his reactions as being both normal and acceptable, given the circumstances. They can make it possible for a person to cope where a self-help strategy has failed.

In exploring these roles for others and the community in this chapter two things need to be borne in mind. First, whilst the needs of a person in crisis are the focus for this chapter, there is also a need to recognize and accept the needs of those who act as helpers. Helper needs are often neglected, since the needs of those in crisis appear to be much greater. But an unhappy or exhausted helper may not be in as strong a position to promote coping as a helper who feels comfortable with his or her role. The second point to note is that the helper benefits from helping often as much as the person in crisis. In part this is because the helper gains some understanding of how a person in crisis can be helped; also, it is because helpers gain a greater understanding of their own coping and own life from their work with others.

This chapter is divided into two sections. The first examines interpersonal helping – helping that involves a small number of persons (at least two). The second involves helping in the context of the community.

Interpersonal Helping

In this section we will describe two forms of helping. The first is a physical form of helping, whilst the second is more directly concerned with counselling.

The physical effects of stress and distress can be considerable. A person in crisis often requires direct help to cope not only with the psychological and social effects of his situation but also with the physical effects. Chapter 2 described a relaxation technique which has been found to be useful as a stress-reduction process. Here we describe a massage system which is equally useful.

Massage is often surrounded with some mystery and innuendo: it has come to be associated with the bordello rather than with helping. Yet massage is an important tool in the relaxation of tense muscles and in many processes which require a person to feel relaxed as well as be relaxed. Few who have experienced massage doubt its value. To a person in crisis, massage is physically comforting. It is also a direct physical way in which one person (the helper) can demonstrate commitment to another (the person in crisis). Massage is an intimate act in so far as it requires such close physical contact between two people; massage is not a sexual act, but a physical process useful for a great many stress conditions.

For massage to be successful, it is necessary for the helper to enable the person to be massaged to relax. Deep breathing, systematically used, can be relaxing. The following relaxation sequence has proved successful on a great many occasions:

The person being massaged should lie flat on the floor, with the stomach pushing down on to the floor; the helper should kneel next to him; it is helpful if the areas to be massaged are readily accessible to the helper (massage is most effective if completed on the body without clothes, but this is clearly a matter for individuals to decide upon – massage can also be useful for a fully clothed person).

The helper should maintain physical contact with the person throughout the massage process, ensuring that the contact is gentle.

The helper asks the person to breathe deeply through the nose and to breathe out through the mouth – the relaxation sequence given on pages 28–29 can be used here, giving particular emphasis to breathing.

We have found it important to continually emphasize to the person that he should not think about the past or about the future, but let himself focus upon the present. We use the following words: 'forget the past for now, don't think of the future, sink yourself more and more into the present moment, let me do the work, let me take charge of your body, concentrate on your breathing, concentrate on what is happening to your body, let me do the work.' This constant reassurance in the early phase of the massage sequence is important not only because of the actual message it gives to the person but also because it establishes the role of the helper firmly in the person's mind.

The helper then needs to proceed to the massage process proper. We have found the following notes of guidance helpful. The notes are written as if for use by a helper:

Apply pressure with your hands – you're not feeling velvet or lace or massaging ice-cream. Clearly, the amount of pressure you apply will vary for different parts of the body – the back will take more pressure than, say, the cheeks or the feet. The rule is to exercise considerable care and to ensure that some pressure is applied.

Relax your hands – there is nothing worse than a tense helper and the tension is usually shown clearly through the hands.

Mould your hands to fit the parts of the body you are working with – don't try to mould the body into a shape you desire or a shape that fits your hands. You're not sculpting clay.

In the massage process try to develop and maintain an evenness of movement and speed. Try to let the person be reassured of your actions and intentions by the pressure, care, evenness of movement and speed and by reassuring verbal messages. In the early moments, this is especially important – it establishes trust.

As the massage continues, do not be afraid to vary the speed and pressure, but ensure that you signal to the person your intentions either verbally or by your actions.

As the helper, it is important that you try to 'tune in' to the body of the person you are helping – what are its strong points, where are its weaknesses, which areas feel thick and which thin, where is the body most/least supple, where do the muscles fall quickly into place after massage? Continually ask yourself these questions and help the person to identify these features of his body.

Use your own weight rather than your muscles to apply pressure on the person. This enables you to relax your hands and prevents you from 'stiffening' your muscles and becoming tense during the massage process.

Actively try not to lose physical contact with the person during the massage.

At the end of the massage, the person should be asked slowly to come round and sit upright.

These notes cannot provide a detailed and thorough description of the massage process. We recommend these texts for further and more thorough descriptions of massage:

Downing, George, (1972): *The Massage Book*. Harmondsworth: Penguin.

Gunther, Bernard (1974): *Sense Relaxation–Blow Your Mind*. London: Macdonald.

One final point about massage. Whilst massage is an important and valuable tool aimed at helping another person relax his body and ease his stress, there is a need for the helper to be careful in his 'use' of another person's body. Care and concern should ensure that the process achieves the objective of relaxing the body and easing distress.

The second set of helping tactics we include under this heading are co-counselling techniques. We should stress here that there are a great many techniques that could be included under this heading. Our choice of co-counselling reflects our experience and training and our understanding of the nature of crisis. This is not a comprehensive textbook of helping techniques, but rather a book offering insights and suggestions which relate directly to crisis experiences.

The basic idea of co-counselling is that peers give assistance to each other. The helper is not someone seeking to use 'expert' skills and knowledge to 'cure' the person in crisis. Rather, the helper is just another person seeking genuinely to help in a way that benefits both the person in crisis and the helper. The aim is to use whatever methods seem appropriate to encourage genuine emotional discharge on the part of the person in crisis. That is, the helper aims to help the person express his crisis pain. There are a number of ways in which this can be done – some of the techniques described on page 150 of the previous chapter are helpful – but there is a systematic process that the helper is seeking to encourage the person to work through. John Rowan, an independent counsellor and consultant in London, describes this process in terms of seven stages. We paraphrase these stages here:

1 In the early stages of helping, the person in crisis resists the release of emotions and concentrates instead upon small issues. What is noticeable about this phase is that the present tends to be viewed in terms of the past and that the person constructs reasons for his circumstances which are external to himself. The helper's task is to encourage the person to see his situation in terms of the present and future and challenge the rationalizations which the person is using to 'defend' his own role in the generation of the crisis or to defend his emotions. The techniques of literal description and role-play may be useful here.

2 At the second stage, the person may begin to show feelings, but will be unwilling to accept them as being 'all his own' and may be unsure about 'how normal' the feelings are. His experience and feelings are held away at arm's length. The helper's task is to help the person accept the feelings that he experiences and displays as his own. Encouragement, reflection of emotions back to the person and

highlighting the way in which the emotions appear to the helper – all these are useful tactics at this stage.

3 At this stage, the person does talk more about his 'self' but does so as if his 'self' was a car or another object or person. The person continues to resist the idea that he is how he feels and that these feelings are a part of him. The helper needs to encourage the person to recognize himself in his descriptions of his own feelings. There is also a need to encourage the person to focus more on the present and the future than upon the past. We have found the use of monodrama (see page 150) especially effective at this stage.

4 The person brings forward more intensive feelings from the past. These may give rise to a recognition that he is more complex as a person than he thought and that there are some (if not many) contradictions in the way that he feels and thinks. This can give rise to either a feeling that there may be more than one way of looking at things or to a feeling that he is 'a bag of worms' in a room without light. This stage needs especially careful handling by the helper. For it is essential that the person be able to see a way through this phase so that an apparent weakness (the contradictions will be seen as weakness by many) becomes a significant strength. What is more, the differences within the person need to be used in a way that loosens the person's view of himself and the world within which he works and lives. Finally, there is a need for the person to be encouraged to explore his expressed feelings in the present rather than the past.

5 At this stage, the person expresses feelings and thoughts more freely than before. What is more, feelings are expressed in the present rather than in the past. The person is also more precise in his expression of thoughts and feelings – it is as if more clarity has descended upon the person and enables him to take more self-responsibility. Whilst this is generally a positive and developmental stage, there is also fear: fear of the consequences of what is bubbling up from beneath the dam inside. The helper has three tasks. First, to help the person recognize the strengths that arise from expressing feelings in the present. Second, the helper needs to enable the person release the feelings that the person is damming up inside himself. Finally, the helper needs to ensure that the person feels fully supported. Some physical forms of helping (relaxation and massage) may be appropriate here.

6 This is a breakthrough stage. The person expresses his thoughts and

feelings in the present – in the 'here and now' – and finds that he is able to work through these feelings and accept them as both his own and as feelings which are legitimate for him to have. There is also a physiological release at this stage – the body reacts to the release of emotions. There may also be a change in the way in which the person views the world. The helper's task is to help the person recognize the stage that he has reached and to consolidate this stage. In particular, the person needs to be enabled to develop trust in his own sense of judgement and his own sensitivity. Direct support is also needed.

7 At this final stage, the person needs to feel able to work on his own feelings in his own time, either on his own or with another person – he should feel able to cope without help. The helper's task is to enable the person to make his own decisions and to act independently. The major task here is to leave the person on his own.

This description of the helping task is not complete without some mention of time and direct action.

The seven stages described here can occur rapidly during crisis or can take a considerable time. The helper needs to be sensitive to the development of the person during this time. In particular, he needs to recognize that the person in crisis may not have much time in which to act or explore. The person, not this model of development, is the focus for helping. The model acts here as a guide to the ideal process.

One of the reasons that many helping services react badly to crisis is that they seek to encourage the person to fully understand the nature of his situation and the reasons for it before action is taken. For example, a battered wife needs some direct practical assistance (i.e., a protected place to stay, financial and emotional support, legal advice and medical attention) before the stages outlined here can begin. The helper should not neglect these important actions – they are often the most important actions to take and if omitted in the search for understanding, the person may not seek help again.

This last point is important for two reasons. First, it reminds helpers that the need to understand and learn through crisis is often secondary to the more immediate need to cope with crisis. Action does speak louder than words when the need is greatest. Second, it stresses to helpers that the person is a part of the community and may therefore benefit from access and use of community resources. Understanding crisis and learning from it is not a priority to the person who has just lost his job, to the person whose husband has just walked out or to the mother whose son has just been killed in a road accident.

To be able to respond to the needs of an individual in terms of actions, there is a need for helpers to be aware of the available resources for the person. Alternatively, there is a need for the helper to be aware of where such information and assistance may be obtained. There is telling evidence that many professional helpers are ignorant of the work of other professional and voluntary workers. This is hardly surprising since there is a massive network of voluntary organizations specializing in different areas of helping and a variety of specialisms within professions. Though not surprising, this situation is not all that helpful. There is a need for closer liaisons between community agencies which offer helping resources and services.

Community Networks for Self-help

The lack of responsiveness to the direct needs of individuals which some have experienced has given rise to a variety of self-help responses at a community level for a variety of circumstances. We have already mentioned the importance of parent organizations for the parents of mentally and physically handicapped children. These are important not only because they offer a source of help to parents, all the more sensitive since the helper and the person in need have many experiences in common (making co-counselling a firm possibility), but also because the helper is able to encourage the person to regard his thoughts and feelings as 'normal', as part of the circumstances and as shared by others who have been through similar experiences. Such organizations are among many. There are others for those experiencing bereavement, for those who have been raped, for those who feel depressed and suicidal and for those whose marriages seem to them to be near collapse or problematic.

So that we might explore some of the principles of these groups and examine the potential of the groups for helping a person cope with crisis, we have chosen to examine here the work of the Mutual Support Network in Wales – an organization of self-help groups which aims to encourage and enable unemployed people to respond to their own situations in their own way. We choose this organization rather than any other simply because we are very familiar with it and its operation: we have been involved in its development as well as in its evaluation.

This network, like many other voluntary groups, has the following kinds of aims:

to enable those experiencing unemployment to meet and work with others undergoing similar experiences;

to encourage unemployed people to take action themselves to gain and control resources which will help them meet their needs; and

to develop skills amongst unemployed people so that their ability to cope increases and so that unemployment can be used productively both for the people and the community.

There is an implicit aim for these groups when they join the network. For the network is a collection of groups sharing the above aims. The network aims to encourage groups to share information, ideas, knowledge and skills between groups so that they may all benefit from the success and failure of others. In short, the network is a self-help grouping of self-help groups which aims to promote mutual aid for mutual benefit.

These kinds of aims may seem no different from the social policy aim of, say, a local municipality or a government. But there are three essential differences. First, the development of services and helping is in the control of those who are in need of help. The services are not delivered to those in need; they are created by those in need. Second, the work of the network is not restricted to alleviating the distress of a particular circumstance, though this is clearly important to its members; the network is also involved in developing skills so that unemployed people, acting alone or collectively, can become more involved in the community in which they live so that they can increase the extent to which they control their own resources within the community. Finally, the responses that arise from self-help are locally determined, not nationally prescribed. This leads to local action being varied by the personalities of the participants and to the nature of local responses being very varied in terms of quality.

These, then, are the ideas behind this network. These ideas are similar to the aims of many other organizations with helping aims and voluntary participation. How do they work in practice?

There are five problems evident in the operation of this network which seem also to apply to other organizations relevant to the crisis events we have described in this book. These are:

1 The problem of imagination: in order to respond to a situation there is a

need to have ideas about possibilities, about what might be done to respond to clear and large-scale need. So often the groups which form the base of the network lack ideas or are stuck with the idea that all that is possible is to use the ideas provided by others. In part this difficulty arises from the lack of experience of those involved in taking responsibility and in part it arises from the enormity of the needs they are seeking to respond to. But by far the greatest difficulty under this heading is the lack of encouragement the individuals have had to explore and experiment in other areas of their lives – they are reluctant to be bold and reluctant to try ideas that seem new.

2 The problem of process: in order to take decisions, some kind of decision-making structures need to be created. Many of the groups find this difficult because there tends to be a 'power struggle' or a conflict of opinion about the best process. What tends to happen is that groups adopt formal committee decision-making procedures which inhibit new ideas and prevent decisive action.

3 The problem of responsibility: some of the groups have been able to develop ideas and make decisions, but shy away from taking the necessary steps to act upon them. It is as if they fear taking full responsibility not only for their idea but also for their circumstances.

4 The problem of professionals: the groups which form the basis of the network turn to professionals for help and guidance at various times, and this is both necessary and potentially productive; there is, however, a tendency for groups to rely too heavily on professionals for advice and to rely too heavily on them for skills and services; this in turn leads some groups to abandon the principle of control by those in need in favour of implementing the plan agreed with the professionals. At the same time, professional community workers become frustrated with the attempts of some groups to develop a strategy and learn the tactics of community responses to unemployment – it is as if the groups are seeking (in the eyes of some professionals at least) to rediscover the wheel.

5 The problem of networking: the groups which form the network begin for their own reasons – they identify local needs which they feel can be met by a particular kind of response. They participate in the network whilst they see it offering advice and services helpful to them in the creation of their group. Once the group is successful and begins to achieve its own aims, there is a tendency for it to reject the idea of networking on the grounds that it offers little for them, not recognizing

that their role in the network has changed from being a group in need of aid to a group in a position to offer aid to another group.

These five difficulties relate to both the individual groups and the collective of groups which is known as the network. The difficulties have a variety of causes. The first is youth – the network is but two years old and many of the groups within it began six to eight months before this chapter was written – so it is early days yet. The second is that the needs that the groups are seeking to respond to are varied and diffuse. There is no one response to unemployment, just as there is no one response to divorce or rape or becoming old. The groups are still working through the idea that they need to create services and resources which can be used in a variety of ways depending upon the needs being displayed by a particular person at a particular time. It is almost as if they are first discovering that standard responses do not lead to standard reactions. Finally, they are learning that they are able to take control of their own resources to meet their own needs. For so many members of the groups this is a novel experience and a painful one – it reminds them of their circumstance of being unemployed and not having control over their own employability.

There are many parallels between these difficulties and those we outlined in the seven-stage description of the underlying co-counselling process above. Indeed, if you work through that description again and insert the phrase 'self-help groups' for the phrase 'the person in crisis' or its equivalent, then you have a good description of the process which many groups will go through. Not all succeed – some fail simply because they cannot identify a response which is satisfactory; others fail because they cannot find a decision-making process; yet others fail because they cannot face the responsibility that community action involves. But many others succeed.

We have laboured this analysis of one particular set of initiatives concerned with unemployment, since the analysis suggests that helpers can have a valuable role in helping individuals and groups overcome some of the difficulties we identify. We suspect, on the basis of personal experience and research, that many help-oriented groups experience these same difficulties. We also suggest that many individuals in these groups experience frustration to the point to which belonging to them can be a crisis in itself. But the point to note is that the person in crisis needs to be enabled to examine this line of response just as much as he needs to be able to examine both self-help and interpersonal responses.

The products of self-help groups in the community are considerable. Not only do the groups, like the Samaritans, Marriage Guidance Councils and others, offer direct help to individuals, but they can also act as powerful campaigners for individual and social needs. For example, pensioner groups can act to help a person cope with the physical and psychological effects of ageing whilst at the same time campaigning for increases in bus concessions, state grants for heating and retirement pensions; groups working for battered wives can offer refuge and advice whilst at the same time campaigning for changes in marital laws relating to physical and mental cruelty; groups working with rape victims can offer practical help and counselling whilst at the same time campaigning for changes in the criminal law relating to rape. Once a person's immediate crisis needs are being met, these groups can offer valuable mutual support and a public/political expression of the needs the person has. This may be important to them – in our experience of working with the unemployed, for example, the political expression of people's needs is a crucial helping tactic.

Conclusion

In writing this book we did not intend to offer a complete guide to helping a person in crisis. Our selection of helping tactics is intended to reflect our own interests and experiences. In this chapter some physical, interpersonal and community responses to crisis have been briefly outlined. Our intention in doing so is to make clear that a person in crisis can be helped by a variety of means – physical, emotional and community-based. The helper's task is not to regard any one method of helping as being 'the only way', but to see the specific needs of the person as the focus which determines the kind of helping that they are able to offer themselves or direct that person to. In the end, the person will accept that which he regards to be most beneficial to him at that time. We should not make the choice of helping tactic a crisis in itself.

REFERENCES

Alberti, R. E. and Emmons, M. L. (1974): *Your Perfect Right – A Guide to Assertive Behaviour*. New York: Impact Press.

Apter, M. J. and Murgatroyd, S. (1976): Concentration, Personality and Programmed Instruction, *Programmed Learning and Educational Technology*, Volume 12, pages 208–215.

Apter, M. J. and Murgatroyd, S. (1980): The Concept of Concentration, *Programmed Learning and Educational Technology*, Volume 17, pages 48–52.

Bayley, M. (1973): *Mental Handicap and Community Care*. London: Routledge & Kegan Paul.

Bergman, K. (1971): The Neurosis of Old Age. In Kay, D. and Walk, A. (eds.): Recent Developments in Psychogeriatrics. *British Journal of Psychiatry*, Special Publication No. 6, pages 35–50.

Boorer, D. R. and Murgatroyd, S. (1973): *Personality and Learning – A Selected Annotated Bibliography*. Wales: MTM Publishing.

Booth, T. A. (1978): From Normal Baby to Handicapped Child, *Sociology*, Volume 12, pages 203–221.

Bolwby, J. (1973): *Separation – Anxiety and Anger*. London: Hogarth Press.

Bowlby, J. (1980): *Loss – Sadness and Depression*. London: Hogarth Press.

Brockelhurst, J. C. et al. (1971): Dysuria in Old Age, *Journal of the American Geriatrics Society*, Volume 19, page 582.

Burgess, A. W. and Holmstrom, L. L. (1979): Adaptive Strategies and Recovery from Rape, *American Journal of Psychiatry*, Volume 136, pages 1278–1282.

Caplan, G. (1964): *Principles of Preventive Psychiatry*. London: Tavistock.

Caplan, G. (1968): *An Approach to Community Mental Health*. New York: Grune Stratton.

Carkhuff, R. (1969): *Helping and Human Relations – A Primer for Lay and Professional Helpers* (2 vols). New York: Holt, Rinehart and Winston.

Challela, M. S. (1981): Helping Parents Cope with a Profoundly Mentally Retarded Child. In Milunsky, A (ed.): *Coping with Crisis and Handicap*. New York: Plenum

Cobb, S. and Kasl, S. (1977): *Termination – The Consequences of Job Loss*. Cincinatti, Ohio: US Department of Health, Education & Welfare.

Coogler, O. J. (1978): *Structured Mediation in Divorce Settlement – A Handbook for Marital Mediators*. Massachusetts: D. C. Heath.

Corney, M. (1981): A Lost Child Lives On, *New Forum*, March, pages 54–56.

Dlugokinski, E. (1977): A Developmental Approach to Coping with Divorce, *Journal of Clinical Child Psychology*, Volume 6, pages 27–30.

Downing, G. (1972): *The Massage Book*. Harmondsworth: Penguin.

Dunham, J. (1981): Resource Checklist to Help You Reduce Tension at Work, *Social Work Today*, Volume 12, No. 29, pages 10–12.

Dustin, R. and George, R. (1973): *Action Counseling for Behaviour Change*. New York: Intext.

Eisenberg, P. and Lazarsfeld, J. (1938): The Psychological Effects of Unemployment, *Psychological Bulletin*, Volume 32, pages 323–345.

Ellis, A. (1962): *Reason and Emotion in Psychotherapy*. New York: Lyle Stuart.

Erikson, E. H. (1950): *Childhood and Society*. New York: W. W. Norton.

Fine, S. (1980): Children in Divorce, Custody and Access Situations – The Contribution of the Mental Health Professional, *Journal of Child Psychology and Psychiatry*, Volume 21, pages 253–261.

Forer, B. (1963): The Therapeutic Value of Crisis, *Psychological Reports*, Volume 13, pages 275–281.

Fox, A. M. (1974): *They Get This Training But They Don't Really Know How You Feel*. USA: National Fund for Research Into Crippling Disease.

Giles, K. and Woolfe, R. (1981): *Personal Change in Adults*. Milton Keynes: Open University Press.

Gordon, T. (1975): *Parent Effectiveness Training*. Boston: Houghton Mifflin.

Gould, R. (1978): *Transformations – Growth and Change in Adult Life*. New York: Simon and Schuster.

Gould, T. and Keynon, J. (1980): *Stories from the Dole Queue*. London: Routledge & Kegan Paul.

Grayfe, C. I., Amies, A. and Ashley, M. (1977): Longitudinal Study of Falls in an Elderly Population, 1 The Incidence of Morbidity, *Age and Ageing*, Volume 6, page 201.

Gunther, B. (1974): *Sense Relaxation–Blow Your Mind*. London: Macdonald.

Haan, C. (1977): *Coping and Defending – Processes of Self-Environmental Organization*. New York: Academic Press.

Harris, T. A. (1973): *I'm OK, You're OK*. London: Pan Books.

Havighurst, R. (1953): *Human Development and Education*. New York: Longman.

Heimler, E. (1969): *Mental Illness and Social Work*. Harmondsworth: Penguin.

Heifetz, L. J. (1977): Professional Preciousness and the Evolution of Parent Training Strategies. In Mittler, P. (ed.): *Research and Practice in Mental Retardation – Care and Prevention*. Manchester: University of Manchester Press.

Hewett, S. with Newson, J. and Newson, E. (1970): *The Family and the Handicapped Child*. London: George Allen and Unwin.

Hopson, B. and Adams, J. (1976): Towards an Understanding of Transition – Defining Some Boundaries of Transition Dynamics. In Adams, J., Hayes, J. and Hopson, B. (eds.): *Transition – Understanding and Managing Personal Change*. London: Martin Robertson.

Hopson, B. and Scally, M. (1980): Change and Development in Adult Life – Some Implications for Helpers, *British Journal of Guidance and Counselling*, Volume 8, pages 175–187.

Horowitz, M. J. (1979): Psychological Responses to Serious Life Events. In Hamilton, V. and Warburn, D. M. (eds.): *Human Stress and Cognition*. London: John Wiley.

Huberman, L. (1974): Looking at Adult Education from the Perspective of the Adult Life Cycle, *International Review of Education*, Volume 20, pages 117–137.

Isreali, N. (1935): Distress in the Outlook of Lancashire and Scottish Unemployed, *Journal of Applied Psychology* , Volume 19, pages 67–69.

Jacobson, G. R. and Lindsay, D. (1979): Screening of Alcohol Problems Among the Unemployed, *Current Alcohol Research*, Volume 7, pages 357–371.

Jahoda, M., Lazarsfeld, P. F. and Zeisel, H. (1971): *Marienthal – The Sociology of an Unemployed Community* (first published 1933). London: Tavistock.

Janis, I. L. (1958): *Psychological Stress*. New York: John Wiley.

Jones, H. A. and Charnley, A. H. (1978): *Adult Literacy – A Study of Its Impact*. Leicester: National Institute for Adult Education.

Komarovsky, M. (1940): *The Unemployed Man and His Family*. New York: Dryden.

Kressel, K., Jaffes, N., et al. (1980): A Typology of Divorcing Couples – Implications for Mediation and the Divorce Process, *Family Process*, Volume 19, pages 101–116.

Lange, A. J. and Jakubowski, P. (1976): *Responsible Assertive Behaviour – Cognitive/Behavioural Procedures for Trainers*. Illinois: Research Press.

Lazarus, R. (1966): *Psychological Stress and the Coping Process*. New York: McGraw Hill.

Lazarus, R. and Launier, R. (1981): Stress Related Transaction Between Person and Environment. In Pervin, L.A. and Lewis, M. (eds.): *Perspectives in Interactional Psychology*. New York: Plenum Press.

Le Masters, E. E. (1965): Parenthood as Crisis. In Parad, H. J. (ed.): *Crisis Intervention – Selected Readings*. New York: Family Service Association of Amercia.

Levinson, D. J. (1978): *Seasons of a Man's Life*. New York: Alfred Knopf.

Little, C. B. (1976): Unemployment – Middle Class Adaptability to Personal Crisis, *Sociological Quarterly*, Volume 17, pages 262–274.

McClelland, D. C. et al. (1953): *The Achievement Motive*. New York: Appleton, Century Croft.

McCormack, M. (1978): *A Mentally Handicapped Child in the Family*. London: Constable.

McNeil, E. (1965): *The Psychology of Being Human*. London: Routledge & Kegan Paul.

Marsden, D. and Duff, E. (1975): *Workless – Some Unemployed Men and Their Families*. Harmondsworth: Penguin.

Maslow, A. H. (1954): *Motivation and Personality*. New York: Harper & Row.

Mead, M. (1949): *Male and Female – Study of the Sexes in a Changing World*. New York: Morrow.

Meichenbaum, D. (1977): *Cognitive-Behaviour Modification – An Integrative Approach*. New York: Plenum Press.

Mezirow, J. (1977): Perspective Transformation, *Studies in Adult Education*, Volume 49, pages 153–164.

Mezirow, J. (1978): *Education for Perspective Transformation – Women's Re-Entry Programs in Community Colleges*. (New York: Center for Adult Education). Columbia: Teachers College Press.

Mills, C. W. (1940): Situated Actions and Vocabularies of Motive, *American Sociological Review*, Volume 5, pages 439–452.

Morris, S. (1981): *Grief – How to Live with It*. London: Routledge & Kegan Paul.

Murgatroyd, S. (ed.) (1980): *Helping the Troubled Child – Interprofessional Case Studies*. London: Harper & Row.

Murgatroyd, S. (1981): *Study Guide and Workbook*. Milton Keynes: The Open University Press.

Murgatroyd, S. (1982): Student Learning Difficulties and the Role of Institutional Support Services. In Martin, J. (ed.): *Student Learning from Different Media in the Open University*. Milton Keynes: The Open University Press.

Murgatroyd, S. and Shooter, M. (1982): Unemployment, The Person and The Family, *Open University* (mimeo).

Nicholson, J. (1980): *Seven Ages*. London: Fontana

Olhansky, S. (1962): Chronic Sorrow – A Response to Having a Mentally Defective Child. In Younghusband, E. (ed.): *Social Work with Families*. London: George Allen and Unwin.

Open University (1979): *The Good Health Guide*. London: Harper & Row.

Osborn, S. M. and Harris, G. G. (1975): *Assertive Training for Women*. Springfield, Ill.: Charles Thomas.

Parad, H. J. and Caplan, G. (1960): A Framework for Studying Families in Crisis, *Journal of Social Work*, Volume 5, pages 3–15.

Parkes, C. M. (1972): *Berevement – Studies of Grief in Adult Life*. London: Tavistock.

Pearlin, L. and Schooler, C. (1978): The Structure of Coping, *Journal of Health and Social Behaviour*, Volume 19, pages 2–21.

Proctor, B. (1978): *Counselling Shop*. London: Burnett Books.

Rapoport, L. (1965): The State of Crisis – Some Theoretical Considerations. In Parad, H. J. (ed.): *Crisis Intervention*. New York: Family Service Association of America.

Roberts, K., Debbon, J. and Noble, M. (1982): Out of School Youth in High Unemployment Areas – An Empirical Investigation, *British Journal of Guidance and Counselling*, Volume 10, pages 1–11.

Rogers, C. (1980): *A Way of Being*. Boston: Houghton Mifflin Co.

Roith, A. I. (1963): The Myth of Parental Attitudes. In Boswell, D. and Wingrove, J. M. (eds.): *The Handicapped Person in the Community*. London: Tavistock

Rowan, J. (1976): *Ordinary Ecstasy*. London: Routledge & Kegan Paul.

Royal College of Physicians (1974): *Report of the Geriatrics Committee Working Group on Strokes*. London: The Royal College of Physicians.

Rutter, M. (1971): Parent Child Separation–Psychological Effects on the Children, *Journal of Child Psychology and Psychiatry*, Volume 12, pages 223–226.

Sanchez-Craig, S. (1976): Cognitive and Behavioural Coping Strategies in the Reappraisal of Stressful Social Situations, *Journal of Counselling Psychology*, Volume 23, pages 7–12.

Schlossberg, N. K. and Leibowitz, Z. (1980): Organisational Support Systems as Buffers to Job Loss, *Journal of Vocational Behaviour*, Volume 17, pages 204–217.

Schutz, W. (1967): *Joy*. New York: Grove Press.

Shady, G. (1978): Coping Styles of Patients with Life Threatening Illness, *Essence*, Volume 2, pages 149–154.

Siann, G., Draper, J. and Cosford, B. (1982): Pupils as Consumers – Perceptions of Guidance and Counselling in a Scottish School, *British Journal of Guidance and Counselling*, Volume 10, pages 51–61.

Smart, R. G. (1979): Drinking Problems Amongst Employed, Unemployed and Shift Workers, *Journal of Medicine*, Volume 21, pages 731–736.

Smith, M. J. (1975): *When I Say No I Feel Guilty*. New York: Dial Press.

Sutherland, S. and Scherl, D. (1970): Patterns of Response Among Victims of Rape, *American Journal of Orthopsychiatry*, Volume 40, pages 503–511.

Tausky, C. and Piedemont, E. B. (1967): Changes in Self-Concept without Psychotherapy, *Journal of Social Psychiatry*, Volume 14, pages 44–49.

Thomas, W. I. (1909): *Source Book for Social Origins*. Boston: Badger Press.

Weiss, R. (1975): *Marital Separation*. New York: Basic Books.

Willis, P. (1979): *Learning to Labour*. London: Gower Press.

Younghusband, E., Birchall, D. and Kellmer-Pringle, M. (eds.) (1970): *Living with Handicap*. London: National Bureau for Co-operation in Child Care.

AUTHOR INDEX

Adams, J., 10
Alberti, E., 154
Apter, M. J., 82

Bergman, K., 82
Boorer, D., 64
Booth, T. A., 92
Bowden, P., 121
Bowlby J., 88, 97, 112
Brockelhurst, J. C., 76
Burgess, A., 127, 130

Caplan, G., 12, 13, 17, 19, 35, 86, 87
Carkhuff, R., 142
Chalella, M. S., 86
Cobb, S., 29, 95
Corney, M., 87

Daws, P., 68
Dlugokinski, E., 56
Downing, G., 159
Duff, E., 96
Dunham, J., 25
Dustin, R., 152

Eisenberg, P., 95
Ellis, A., 143, 147
Emmons, M. L., 154
Erikson, E., 42

Fine, S., 60
Fitzgibbon, G., 25
Forer, B., 20
Fox, A. M., 91
Freud, S., 105

George, R., 152

Giles, K., 44
Gordon, T., 87
Gould, R., 43, 95
Gryfe, C. I., 77
Gunther, B., 159

Harris, G. G., 154
Havighurst, R., 43
Heifitz, L. J., 88, 89
Heimler, E., 91
Hewett, S., 84, 85
Holmstrom, V., 127, 130
Hopson, B., 10, 42
Horowitz, M. J., 18, 19, 20
Huberman, L., 44, 45

Israeli, N., 95

Jacobson, C. R., 95
Jahoda, M., 95
Janis, I. L., 105

Karl, S., 95
Keynon, J., 95
Komarovsky, M., 95
Kressel, K., 49

Laye, A., 153
Launier, R., 24
Lazarfeld, J., 95
Lazarus, R., 22, 24
Leibowitz, Z., 97
Levinson, D. J., 43
Lindsay, D., 95
Little, C. B., 97

Marsden, D., 96

McClelland, D. C., 67
McCormack, M., 88
McNeil, E., 110
Mead, M., 110
Mezisow, J., 46
Morris, S., 110
Murgatroyd, S., 64, 65, 66, 94, 101, 102,
    110

Nicholson, J., 44

Olshansky, S., 88
Osborn, S. M., 154

Parad, H. J., 14
Parkes, C. M., 25, 88, 113
Pearlin, L., 25, 26, 34
Piedemont, E. B., 95

Roberts, K., 68, 70
Rogers, C., 16, 78, 79

Rowan, J., 160
Rutter, M., 61

Scally, M., 42
Scherl, D., 126
Schlossberg, N. K., 97
Schooler, C., 25, 26, 34
Shooter, M., 94, 101–104
Siann, G., 70
Smart, R. G., 95
Sutherland, S., 126

Tausky, C., 95
Thomas, W. J., 11

Weiss, R., 55
Willis, P., 68
Wood, P. H. N., 74
Woolfe, R., 44

Younghusband, E., 85

SUBJECT INDEX

Acceptance, 59, 92, 117, 145
Accidents, 73, 77
Accurate understanding, 58
Active rehearsal, 90
Actual self, 70
Acute reactions, to rape, 127
Adjustment needs, 56
Adolescence, 63ff
Adolescent development, 60
'Adult' ego state, 32
Advocacy role of helpers, 4, 95
Ageing, 41, ff
Aggression, 29, 121, 152
Alcoholism, 95, 98, 113
Ambivalence in marriage, 49
American Journal of Psychiatry, 130
Amputation, 106
Anger, 53, 61, 82, 88, 132
Anorexia nervosa, 8
Anti-social criminal rapist, 121
Anticipatory coping, 25, 26
Anxiety, 11, 17, 58, 59, 117, 126, 127,
    128, 143
Anxiety-depression, 1
Arousal, 12, 35, 142
Arthritis, 29, 95
Assertiveness, 23, 29, 34, 67, 68, 152–153
Association, 150
Atonement, 113
Attachment, 55
'Autistic' divorcing couple, 56
Awareness, 99, 113

Back aches, 61
Battered women, 162
Benefit nights, 90, 140
Bereavement, 25, 87, 156, 163

Biography, 25
Biological maturation, 41
Bone-brittleness, 74
Bondage, 16
Bonus systems in self-contracting, 152
Boston, 130
Brain functioning, 75
British League Against Rheumatism, 74
'Broken-record' technique, 153
Buffer coping, 25, 34
Buggery, 123, 124
Burial, 86, 99, 114

Cancer, 106
Careers choice, 68
Careers worker, 8
Catch-22, 65
Cathartic experiences, 99
Change, 42
Change as function of coping, 22
Changes in appearance, 73
Checklists, 58
Cheese, 142
Chemists, 77
Child ego-state, 32
Children in divorce, 60
Chocolate, 142
Chronic sorrow, 88
Circulatory system and age, 75
Citizens rights, 46
Clear expectations in self-contracting, 152
Clergy, 79, 111
Co-counselling, 160–163
Cognitive restructuring, 37, 59, 119, 151
Cognitive state, 17
Community, 66, 79, 162
Completion, 20, 112

Concentration, 17, 22
Conceptual skills, 75
Conflict in marriage, 49
Confrontation, 5, 16, 141, 142, 160
Congruence, 70
Consolidation, 57
Conversation management skills, 30
Coping skills training, 97
Coping strategies, 10, 14, 17, 25, 92, 114
Coping tactics, 1, 25, 114
Coping threshold, 14
*Coping with Crisis Research and Training
    Group*, 1, 94
Coronary failure, 95, 108
Counselling, 18, 23, 33, 95, 132, 146, 157,
    167
Counsellor, 89, 144, 160
Creativity, 75
Crisis levels, 14
Crisis management strategy, 26, 37
Critical parent, 31
Critical self-reflection, 47
Custody of children in divorce, 53
Cystic fibrosis, 89

Dating, 129
Deafness, 83
Death, 7, 9, 10, 18, 35, 41, 105, 140, 148,
    156
Decision making skills, 27, 68
Delinquency, 65
Denial, 18, 19, 35, 57, 88, 98, 113, 130
Denmark, 70
Dental care, 74
Dependence, 59, 64, 80, 148
Depersonalisation, 97
Depression, 58, 59, 82, 88, 97, 98, 100,
    103, 113, 119, 132, 148
Development, 42
Developmental charges, 41
Developmental crises, 139
Diabetes, 95
Diet, 100
Digestion, 73, 74, 82
'Direct conflict' type in divorce, 51
Disbelief, 88
'Disengaged type' in divorce, 52
Disengagement, 45
Disfigurement, 111
Disorganisation, 114
Disorientation, 114
Distress, 145, 148

Divorce, 9, 24, 41, 48, 140, 147, 156
Divorce settlements, 51, 54
Doctors, 8, 76, 89, 92, 129, 140
Dress, 69
Drive-reduction, 12
Drug abuse, 77, 115
Drug dependence, 108

Eccentricities, 56
Eclectic forms of helping, 155
Educational counsellors, 68
Educational guidance workers, 68
Ego-grams, 33, 34
Emotional discharge, 160
Emotional well-being, 101
Empathy, 2, 59, 66, 70, 101, 137, 140
England, 122
'Enmeshed type' of divorcing couple, 49,
    50
'Enthusiast' view of adolescence, 66
Entrapment, 148
Equilibrium, 12, 13, 87
Estrangement, 105
Examinations, 144
'Explosive type' rapist, 121
Extra-marital sex, 128

Facilitating charge, 67
Fainting, 144
Fantasy, 98, 118
Fantasy search, 112
Fear of failure, 67
Fear of men, 131
Fear of sex, 131
Fellatio, 123
Feminism, 111
Fidelity, 49
Financial aspects of divorce, 55
Financial status, 48
Fitness, 100
'Fogging', 154
Formal organisations, 14
Fragmentations, 64
'Freezing' strategy, 102, 103
Frustration, 59
Funerals, 110

Gangrene, 117
Genuineness, 70, 137, 140
Goals, 13
Good Health Guide, 142
Gout, 85

Grief, 36
Grief-work, 35, 87, 97, 98, 105, 106, 112
Guilt, 17, 59, 88, 90, 115, 129, 132

Hardening of the arteries, 75
*Harvard Laboratory of Human
    Development*, 70
Headaches, 71
Health visitors, 89
Heart attack (see also strokes), 27
Helper as advocate (see also advocacy), 86
Helper availability, 116
Helping contract, 54, 57, 59
Helping The Troubled Child, 110
Helplessness (see also learned
    helplessness), 13, 119
Homeostasis, 12
Homosexual rape, 120
Hopelessness, 58
Hostility, 90
Housing, 56, 80
Humiliation, 122
Hunger, 12
Hypertension, 95
Hypothermia, 74, 80

Ideal self, 69, 80
Identity, 45, 55, 58, 59, 98, 112
Illness, 9, 12, 73
Immediate memory, 81
Implicit assumptions in assertiveness, 153
Income reduction, 79
Incontinence, 76
Inflation, 80
Information giving, 89
Inheritance, 118
Insight, 34
Integration, 57, 126, 131
Intellectual abilities, 78
Intellectual processes, 82
Intercourse, 123
Intrusion, 19
Irrational beliefs, 143ff
Isolation, 12, 85, 102

Job-loss grieving, 99
Job-skills, 46

Lassa-fever, 106
'Latent homosexual type' rapist, 121
Lawyers, 54
Learned helplessness, 98

Learner-worker role, 67
Learning, 78, 81
Legal charges in rape, 128
Leisure, 97
Lethargy, 119
Levels of crisis, 17
Life-cycle, 43, 44
Life-course, 44
Literal descriptions, 150, 160
Liverpool, 68
London, 160
Long-term memory, 81
Long-term unemployed, 94
Loss, 41, 91, 97, 105, 109, 112
Leukemia, 106, 117

Management function of coping, 22
Marriage, 26, 45, 50, 55, 107, 129
Marriage guidance, 50, 55, 140, 146
Masectomy, 111
Massage, 157, 160, 161
Masturbation, 124
Mandsley Hospital, London, 121
Meditation, 25
Melancholia, 109
Memory, 75, 78, 81
Mental cruelty, 167
Mental handicap, 84
Mental health, 11
Mental illness, 121
Mental retardation, 117
Mid-life crisis, 41
Migraine, 142
Minimisation, 130
Monitoring, 152
Monodrama, 150, 156, 161
Morbidity, 82
Mutual aid, 94, 156
Mutual Support Network in Wales, 156, 163
Mutuality, 141

National Institute for Mental Health, 25
Need for intimate relationships, 42
Negative emotions, 117
Networking, 164
Normal development, 1
Normalization, 92
Normative grief, 116
Northern Ireland, 68
Nursery school, 56
Nursing, 67
Nursing homes, 72

'Nurturing' parent, 69

Open University, 1, 44, 73, 94, 142
Openess, 16, 49
Opportunity awareness, 113
Orientation, 57
Outcry, 18, 19
Outward adjustment, 130

Pace of social change, 45
Pain, 26
Para-professional volunteers, 90
Paradoxical statements, 154
Paralysis, 76
Parent education, 46
Parent ego-states, 31
Parental roles, 86
Parents, 128
Part-time work, 72
Pathological feelings, 91
Pension rights, 80
Perception, 75
Persecuted view of adolescence, 65
Personal differences, 49
Personal rights, 29
Phobias, 131
Physical changes due to age, 73
Physical handicap, 84ff
Physical stress, 142
Play groups, 56
Police, 8, 129
Politics, 45, 104
Positive comparison, 36
Post-mortem, 18, 107
Poverty, 99
Prayer, 25
Pre-marital sex, 128
Pregnancy, 26, 107, 131
Problem solving skill, 54
Professionalism, 2
Projection, 2, 92
Psycho-prophylaxis, 26
Psychological development, 63
Psychological distress, 95

Questioning skills, 154

Rabies, 106
Rape, 7, 10, 24, 27, 41, 120, 140, 163
Rape Crisis Centre Workers, 129, 140
Re-finding, 98

Re-loss, 98
Re-marriage, 147
Reachable goals, 152
Reaction-formation, 35
Recrimination, 56
Redundancy, 8, 27
Reflection, 153, 160
Rehousing, 72
Reitterative skills, 30
Rejection, 141
Relaxation routine, 28, 34
Relaxation training, 27, 142, 161
Religion, 46
Remorse, 90
Repeated assertion, 153
Repetition, 150
Repression, 35, 58, 59, 61
Residential care, 80
Respect, 153
Responsiveness to temperature, 74
Retirement, 46, 72, 79
Reversal, 98, 113
Role, 45, 140
Role-play, 59, 160
Royal College of Physicians, 76

Sadness, 61, 82, 88
Samaritans, 11, 167
Sanctions, 152
Schooling, 56
Scotland, 70
Searching, 98, 112
Second marriage, 148
Selective attention, 118
Selective ignoring, 35
Self-awareness, 113
Self-care, 57
Self-concept, 64, 69
Self contracts, 57, 151
Self-esteem, 21, 69, 95
Self-help, 93, 95, 141, 151, 157, 164, 166
Self-protective skills, 30
Separation, 9, 10
Separation-individuation, 63, 100
Severance pay, 97
Sex aggressive diffusion rapist, 121
Sex roles, 64, 68
Sexual assault, 120
Sexual behaviour, 69
Sexual exploration, 56
Sexual fantasies, 8
Sexual fetish, 15, 17

Sexual repression of women, 121
Shame, 61, 90
Short-term memory, 81
Short-term residential care, 86
Situational crisis, 139
Skill sharing, 2
Sleep, 82, 109, 119, 142
Social change, 41
Social expectations, 64, 68
Social isolation, 99
Social mobility, 80
Social support, 80, 97, 111
Social workers, 89, 90, 91, 140
Specificity, 152
Status, 69
Steel Corporation of Wales, 8
Stress, 11, 18, 24, 25, 29, 35, 69, 74, 147, 157
Stroke, 76
Structured mediation in divorce, 53
Suicide, 17, 163
Supression, 130
Surgery, 35, 106

Television violence, 10
Temperature, 73
Tension, 11, 13, 14, 16, 19, 37, 142
Terminal illness, 10, 82, 106
Theft, 124
Therapy, 144
Tranquilizers, 116
Transactional analysis, (TA), 27, 31, 59
Transcendental meditation, 27, 34

Transition learning, 41, 67, 113, 139
Trial separation, 52
Trial and error learning, 13, 14

Unemployment, 41, 68, 94ff, 164
United Kingdom, 79
United States of America, 48, 70, 79, 130
University of Bath, 25
University of Berkeley, 22
Unpleasant feelings, 143
Unreal expectations, 57

Vandalism, 65
Venereal disease, 128
'Victim' view of adolescence, 65
Vietnam, 146
Vindictiveness, 19
Violence, 123
Vocabulary of motives, 91
Vocational competence, 46
Volunteering, 163–164
Vulnerability in rape, 124

Warmth, 59, 70, 137, 140
Withdrawal, 98
Work, 45
Work of worry, 43, 105, 117
Worry, 59
Worthlessness, 17

Yoga, 25, 96
Young adulthood, 45
Youth unemployment, 63, 100